Asa. Hull

Gospel Praise Book

A Collection of choice gems of sacred song suitable for church service,

gospel praise meetings, and family devotions

Asa. Hull

Gospel Praise Book
A Collection of choice gems of sacred song suitable for church service, gospel praise meetings, and family devotions

ISBN/EAN: 9783337181789

Printed in Europe, USA, Canada, Australia, Japan

Cover: Foto ©Lupo / pixelio.de

More available books at **www.hansebooks.com**

GOSPEL PRAISE BOOK

A COLLECTION OF

CHOICE GEMS OF SACRED SONG

SUITABLE FOR

Church Service, Gospel Praise Meetings,

AND

FAMILY DEVOTIONS.

BY

ASA HULL,

Author of " Pilgrim's Harp," " Grove Songs," " Devotional Chimes," " Hull's Temperance Glee Book," " Garlands of Praise," " Wreath of Praise," etc., etc.

NEW YORK:

Published by D. W. KNOWLES, 240 Fourth Avenue.

BOSTON:

JAMES P. MAGEE, 38 Bromfield Street.

CINCINNATI, O.: | CHICAGO, ILL.:
JOHN CHURCH & CO. | **ROOT & SON'S MUSIC CO.**

This little volume of Sacred Songs is sincerely dedicated to the Churches of the United States of America, by the

Author

New York, July 1st, 1879.

———◆———

Let the people praise Thee, O God ; Let all the people praise Thee. O let the nations be glad and sing for joy. *Psalms* lxvii, 3 and 4.

Praise the Lord with harp ; Sing unto Him a new song ; Play skilfully with a loud noise. *Psalms* xxxiii, 2 and 3.

———◆———

Sing on, my soul, thy mission prove,
Sing sweetly on that song of love :
Uphold the right, condemn the wrong,
And triumph by the power of song.

THE RIVEN ROCK.

Words by MARY D. JAMES.

Music by ASA HULL.

1, { Be - hold the Rock, the smit - ten Rock! With-in its rift - ed side }
{ I've found a bless - ed ref - uge, where I may se - cure - ly hide. }

2. { Tho' thund'ring Si - nai's ter - rors sound Ap-pall - ing to the ear, }
{ Con-cealed with-in the cleft, I'm safe: No dan - ger will I fear. }

CHORUS.

O, the Rock, the Rock, the riv - en Rock! My Sav-iour cru - ci - fled;

No oth - er shel - ter is se - cure But Je - sus' wounded side.

3.
Jesus, dear refuge of my soul!
My hope, my joy, my rest ;
Confiding in Thy changeless love,
I am supremely blest.
Chorus.—O, the Rock, etc.

4.
My peace, unbroken by life's storms,
While I in Christ abide,
My spirit rests in sweetest calm,
As in the Cleft I hide.
Chorus.—O, the Rock, etc.

COME, O COME TO JESUS.

Words by Mrs. E. C. ELLSWORTH.   Music by J. H. TENNEY.

1. I have found the Sav-iour precious, He has fill'd my soul with cheer ;
2. I have found the Sav-iour precious, He is fair - est of the fair ;

I have found Him kind and gracious, And would tell it far and near.
He is chief a - mong ten-thousand, O that all His grace may share.

CHORUS.

Come, O come,..... ... dear friends, to Je - - sus, Since His
Come, O come, dear friends, to Je-sus, Come, O come, dear friends, to Jesus, Since His

love....... is full and free ; In His hand........ is life e -
love is full and free, is life e-ter - nal, is

ter - nal, There's e - nough....... for you and me..........
life e - ter - nal, There's e-nough for you and me, yes, e-nough for you and me.

for you and me...........

Music by G. F. Root.

1. My days are glid - ing swift - ly by, And I, a pil - grim stranger,
2. We'll gird our loins, my brethren dear, Our dis - tant home dis - cern-ing,

Would not de - tain them as they fly! Those hours of toil and dan - ger.
Our ab - sent Lord has left us word, Let ev - 'ry lamp be burn-ing.

CHORUS.

For O! we stand on Jordan's strand, Our friends are pass - ing o - ver;

And just be - fore, the shi - ning shore We may al - most dis - cov - er.

3 Should coming days be cold and dark,
   We need not cease our singing ;
   That perfect rest naught can molest,
   Where golden harps are ringing. *Cho.*

4 Let sorrow's rudest tempests blow,
   Each cord on earth to sever ;
   Our King says, Come, and there's our [home,
   Forever, O, forever ! *Cho.*

CONCLUSION OF **COME, O COME**, OPPOSITE PAGE.

3 I have found the Saviour precious,
   Never failing in my need ;
   For my hungry soul providing,
   Jesus is a friend indeed.
   Chorus.—Come, O come, etc.

4 I have found the Saviour precious,
   Rock of ages, cleft for all ;
   O then find that place of safety,
   For there's room for great and small.
   Chorus.—Come, O come, etc.

BEAUTIFUL STAR, SHINE ON.

Words by E. Rinehart.

Music by Asa Hull.

1. On storm - y seas I sail my bark, Nor fear for once the billows dark ;
2. In dark - est night, when all is drear, For that bright Star my bark I steer ;

For streaming from the skies a - far Shines out the bright, the morning star.
Its rays out-shine the sil - ver moon, And bright-er yet than gold-en noon.

CHORUS. *Rep. pp ad lib.*

Shine on, ... shine on,.... shine on, O beau - ti - ful, beau-ti-ful star ;
Shine on,........ ... shine on, shine on,

Shine on,...... shine on,..... shine on, O beautiful star................
Shine on,........ shine on, shine on, O beau-ti-ful star.

3 When on the crested wave I'm borne,
Amid the tumult of the storm ;
Or, when the sea is calm and still,
'Tis by that light I read God's will.
Chorus.—Shine on, etc.

4 Beyond the main a joyous band
Is waiting on the shining strand,
To welcome to that peaceful shore
My little bark, its perils o'er.
Chorus.—Shine on, etc.

Words by Rev. T. J. Shelton. Music by J. H. Rosecrans.

1. Come and join the march for glo-ry, Bear a no-ble part;
2. Take the Bi-ble precious treas-ure, Faith shall be our shield;

Bring the bless-ed "old, old sto-ry," Home to ev-'ry heart.
Fol-low Je-sus, do His pleas-ure, Nev-er, nev-er yield.

CHORUS.

Take the fort........ of sin and darkness, Je-sus leads us on ;......
take the fort   on, leads us on ;

Take the fort ...... for Christ our Saviour, And win a star-ry crown.
take the fort

3 Take the helmet of Salvation,
  And the Spirit's Sword ;
  Bear the truth to ev'ry nation,—
  Battle for the Lord.
    Cho.—Take the fort, etc.

4 God of battles will defend us,
  To our help will come ;
  Angel guards will e'er attend us,
  And conduct us home.
    Cho.—Take the fort, etc.

THE CITY OF GOD.

Words by Newton.　　　　　　　　　　　　　　　　Music by Asa Hull.

1. Glo - rious things of thee are spok - en, Zi - on, cit - y of our God;
2. On the Rock of A - ges founded, What can shake thy sure repose?

He, whose word can - not be brok-en, Formed thee for His own a-bode.
With sal - va - tion's walls sur-round-ed, Thou mayst smile at all thy foes.

CHORUS.

Zi - on, Zi - on, beau - ti-ful Zi - on, Zi - on, cit - y of our God;
beau-ti-ful, beauti - ful Zi - on,

He, whose word can - not be brok-en, Formed thee for His own a-bode.

3 Round each habitation hov'ring,
　See the cloud and fire appear!
For a glory and a cov'ring,
　Showing that the Lord is near.

4 He who gives us daily manna,
　He who listens when we cry,
Let Him hear the loud hosanna
　Rising to His throne on high.

Copyright, 1879, *by* Asa Hull.

Words by FANNY CHURCH.　　　　　　Music by J. H. TENNEY. Arranged.

1. O songs of faith that pil-grims sing! To you our hearts for-ev-er cling;
2. O songs of love that an-gels sing! What peace and joy your sweet notes bring;
3. And now, O joy! at last, at last The years of toil and woe are past,

You guide us where the saints have trod, You lead us to the throne of God.
They float so sweet-ly down the way That leads us up to end-less day.
And Zi-on's gold-en gate appears; We pass for aye from grief and tears.

REFRAIN.

O mu-sic soft! O mu-sic sweet! Borne up-ward by your song;
O mu-sic soft! O mu-sic sweet! With heav-en in the strain;
O mu-sic soft! O mu-sic sweet! We lay our bur-den down

Tho' storms of time a-round us beat, The weak-est heart grows strong.
Our wait-ing ears your sweet songs greet, They calm our wea-ry pain.
For ev-er-more at Je-sus' feet, And there re-ceive our crown.

MOUNT OF BLESSING.

Words by EDGAR PAGE.   Music by ASA HULL.

1. I've been up the Mount with my Lord to-day, In blessed commun-ion a-
2. He told of His own, His most gracious love, And pleasures prepared for
3. He then brought me down by the waters still, To the flow-'ry vale where the

long the way; Tho' He is a King and of roy-al birth, He deigns to lift
me a-bove; My heart was a-glow with His blessed word, Because of the
song-birds trill; In the pastures green I was led a-long, Till my soul was

Ritard. CHORUS.

up.... the weak ones of earth. O it is a glo-rious place to be, And
pre - sence of Christ my Lord.
filled with joy and with song.

O what a won-der it is to me, That my Saviour goes with me as I

Ritard.

jour - ney a - long, And fills my soul with joy and with song.

Revised and Harmonized by Asa Hull.

Words and Melody by Rev. E. H. Long.

Moderato.

1. Draw me, Sa-viour, near-er, Near-er and near-er to Thee;
2. As the ea - gles soar - ing, High-er and high-er as - cend,

Let me see still clos - er, All Thy love for me.
Thus, while Thee a - dor - ing, Up - ward I would tend.

Freed from self, and whol-ly Thine, Let me in Thy beau-ty shine;
Far from earth and sin a - way, Near - er heav-en's per - fect day;

Rit.

While I sing, O, may I be Drawn still clos-er, clos-er to Thee,
E - ven now, O, may I be Drawn still clos-er, clos-er to Thee,

A tempo.

Clos - er, clos - er, clos-er to Thee.
Clos - er, clos - er, clos-er to Thee.

3 As the river flowing
Daily draws nearer the sea,
Thus may I keep going,
Till I'm lost in Thee.
E'er advance and grow in grace,
Till I see Thee face to face ;
Then I'll sing eternally,
Drawn still closer, closer to Thee,
Closer, closer, closer to Thee.

Words by Rev. J. Milton Akers.   Music by Asa Hull.

1. Sing on, my soul, thy mission prove, Sing sweet-ly on that song of love ;
2. Sing on, my soul, the glad re-frain, Thy mis-sion can - not prove in vain ;

Up-hold the right, condemn the wrong, And triumph by the pow'r of song.
Sing out the false in heart and mind, Sing er - rors out of ev - 'ry kind.

CHORUS. *Rep. pp ad lib.*

Sing on,.......... sing on,.......... sing on, my soul, sing sweetly
Sing on, sing sweet-ly on, Sing on, sing sweet-ly on,

on ;   Sing on,............ sing on,............ Till
on, sing sweet-ly on ; Sing on, sing sweet-ly on, Sing on, sing sweet-ly on,

all of sin and self has gone.
     has gone.

3 Sing in the beautiful and true,
   O sing that song forever new ;
   Sing in the reign of faith and love,
   Sing sweetly on, thy mission prove.

4 Sing out the grov'ling and the low,
   Sing vices out that ever grow ;
   Sing in the pure, the noble, high,
   Sing graces in that never die.

BOUNDLESS LOVE.

Words by E. J. Coffin. Music by Asa Hull.

1. O the love of Christ is boundless, Wid-er than the wid-est sea;
2. O the love of Christ is deep-er Than the darkest, black-est sin;

Reaching to the vil-est sin-ner, It hath found out e-ven me.
In the wel-come "who-so-ev-er" E-ven I am counted in.

REFRAIN.

E-ven me, yes! e-ven me; It hath found out e-ven me.
E-ven I, yes! e-ven I; E-ven I am counted in.

Hal-le-lu-jah! hal-le-lu-jah! It hath found out e-ven me.
Hal-le-lu-jah! hal-le-lu-jah! E-ven I am count-ed in.

3 O the love of Christ is higher
Than our aspirations are;
And it bids each soul come nearer,
Even me who strayed so far.
Even me, yes! even me;
Even me who strayed so far.
Hallelujah! hallelujah!
Even me who strayed so far.

4 O this love is everlasting,
Naught has power to break the tie;
One with Christ, I all inherit,
I am His, yes! even I.
Even I, yes! even I;
I am His, yes! even I.
Hallelujah! hallelujah!
I am His, yes! even I.

THE SACRED STREAM.

Music by Asa Hull.

Solo.—*Allegro.*

QUARTETTE.

mp

mf

1. There is a stream, whose gen - tle flow Sup - plies the cit - y

*pp

DUET.

mp

of........ our God;........ Life, love, and joy, still glid - ing
cit - y of our God;..........

p

QUARTETTE.

mf

through, And wa - t'ring our di - vine........ a - bode......
di - vine a - bode........

FULL CHORUS.

mf

Life, love, and joy, still glid - ing through, And wa - t'ring our di-

vine...... a - bode, And wa - t'ring our di - vine a - bode.
di - vine a - bode,

Cres.

ff

* Small notes may be sung to the syllable "*la*," in the absence of an instrument.
Copyright, 1879, *by* Asa Hull.

Words by Rev. E. A. Hoffman.

Music by J. H. Tenney.

1. My Sav - iour guides me in the way That leads to realms of end - less day ;
2. My Sav - iour is my dear - est friend, And He will love me to the end ;
3. My Sav - iour nev - er leaves my side, He knows what sorrows will be-tide ;

And tho' His plans I can-not tell, Yet, Je - sus do - eth all things well.
Tho' troubles come, in peace I dwell, For Je - sus do - eth all things well.
And tho' rough bil-lows o'er me swell, I know He do - eth all things well.

CHORUS.

O love, no mor - tal tongue can tell ! O love, no hu - man power can quell !

Ritard.

What - e'er be - tide, in peace I dwell, For Je - sus do - eth all things well.

Copyright, 1879, by Asa Hull.

CONCLUSION OF **THE SACRED STREAM,** OPPOSITE PAGE.

2 That sacred stream, Thine holy word,
   'That all our ‖: raging :‖ fear controls ;
  Sweet peace Thy promises afford,
   And give new strength to ‖: fainting :‖
  souls.

3 Loud may the troubled ocean roar ;
   In sacred peace ‖: our souls :‖ abide ;
  While every nation, every shore,
   Trembles and dreads the ‖: swelling :‖
  tide.

WALK IN THE LIGHT.

Words by Asa Hull.

Music by Geo. C. Hugg.

1. Walk in the light the Lord hath giv'n, To guide thy steps a-right;
2. Walk in the light of gos-pel truth, That shines from God's own word;

His ho-ly Spir-it sent from heav'n Can cheer the dark-est night.
A light to guide in ear-ly youth The faith-ful of the Lord.

CHORUS.

Walk......... in the light,............. Walk......... in the
Walk in the light, in the beau-ti-ful light of God, Walk in the light, in the

light,......... ..... Walk........ in the light,.............
beau-ti-ful light of God, Walk in the light, in the beau-ti-ful light of God,

Walk in the light, the light of God.

3 Walk in the light! tho' shadows dark
   Like spectres cross thy way;
 Darkness will flee before the light
   Of God's eternal day.—*Chorus.*

4 Walk in the light! and thou shalt know
   The love of God to thee;
 The fellowship so sweet below,
   In heav'n will sweeter be.—*Chorus.*

Words and Music by Asa Hull.

1. There's an o-pen fount in Zi-on, Where the liv-ing wa-ters flow;
   Ho! ye, ev-'ry son and daugh-ter, Life e-ter-nal ye may have;

Opened free by Ju-dah's Li-on, There the thirst-y soul may go.
Come and drink the liv-ing wa-ter; Come and drink, thy soul shall live.

REFRAIN.

Come and drink, thy soul shall live,.... Come and drink, thy soul shall live;
shall live, shall live;

Come, and drink the liv-ing wa-ter, Come and drink, thy soul shall live.

2 He that drinketh thirsteth never,
  For his soul is satisfied ;
He shall dwell in peace forever,
  And sit down at Jesus' side.
Ho! ye, ev'ry one that thirsteth,
  Christ can living water give ;
You can have it without money,
  Only drink, thy soul shall live.
Only drink, thy soul shall live, etc.

3 To that fountain ever flowing,
  Whosoever will, may come ;
Endless life on all bestowing,
  Whosoever will, there's room.
Pilgrim, haste to Zion's mountain,
  Everlasting life receive ;
Hie thee to that flowing fountain,
  Drink, O drink, thy soul shall live,
Drink, O drink, thy soul shall live, etc.

WHERE ARE THE HARVESTERS?

Words by MARY D. JAMES.

Music by ASA HULL.

1. Lo! the rip - en'd grain is wav - ing, Read - y for the har-vest hands;
2. Who is read - y to o - bey Him? Who, re-spon - sive to His word,

Ritard.

Call - ing loud - ly for more la - b'rers, See! the bless-ed Mas - ter stands.
Now will go in - to the har - vest, Glad to la - bor for their Lord?

CHORUS.

Who is read - y for the harvest? Who will work for dy-ing souls to-day?
Who is rea - dy — Who will work

Ritard.

Who will speak for the blessed Mas-ter? Who will labor, watch, and pray?
Who will speak

3 Workers, see, your Lord is standing,
Looking with benignant smile ;
Watching all your faithful labors,
Giving you good cheer the while !

4 Say, is not the work a pleasure ?
Is not toil a present joy ?
Is not labor rest, when Jesus
Smiles upon your blest employ ?

5 Who can tell the wealth of blessing,
Crowning that rich "harvest-home,"
When within the heavenly portals,
All the faithful lab'rers come ?

6 O, the rapture ! O, the glory !
O, the wondrous feast of love !
When the sowers and the reapers
Gather in their house above.

Words by Rev. H. R. Trickett.   Music by J. H. Rosecrans.

1. Saved ! saved ! saved ! saved by the blood of the Lamb,— Yield-ing at last to the soul-sav-ing word, Owning that Je-sus is Saviour and Lord, Trust-ing a-lone in His name.

2. Saved ! saved ! saved ! ransomed from death and the grave ; Strong was the arm that redeemed me from sin, Precious the blood that has washed my soul clean, Great was the grace that for-gave.

Saved!..............

CHORUS.

An-gels rejoice o'er the dead made alive, Swelling the cho-rus in praise of His name ; Sing, O my soul, for now thou art free !

Rit. ad lib.

Saved by the blood of the Lamb.

3.
Saved! saved! saved! numbered with those who [believe ;
Written my name in the Lamb's book of life ;
Armed and equipped for the war and the strife,
Daily His grace I receive.—*Chorus.*

4.
Saved ! saved ! saved ! never from Christ will [I roam :
Death with its fetters cannot bind me fast,
Mansions of glory await me at last,
Angels will welcome me home.—*Chorus.*

ONE DAY NEARER HOME.

Words from "S. S. Gem," by permission.

Music by Asa Hull.

1. O'er the hills the sun is set-ting, And the eve is draw-ing on;
2. Worn and wea-ry, oft the pil-grim Hails the set-ting of the sun,

Slow-ly drops the gen-tle twi-light, For an-oth-er day is gone.
For the goal is one day near-er, And his jour-ney near-ly done;

Gone for aye—its race is o-ver; Soon the dark-er shades will come;
Thus we feel when o'er life's des-ert Heart and san-dal-sore we roam;

Still 'tis sweet to know at eve-ning That we're one day near-er home.
As the twi-light gathers o'er us, We are one day near-er home.

REFRAIN. *Repeat pp ad lib.*

Near - er, near - er, One day near-er home; .....
Near - er, near - er, near - er, near - er, near-er home;

Near - er, near - er, One day near - er home.......

Near - er, near - er, near - er, near - er, near - er home.

3 Nearer home! yes, one day nearer
   To our Father's house on high,
   To the green fields and the fountains
   Of the land beyond the sky;
   For the heavens grow brighter o'er us,
   And the lamps hang in the dome,
   And our tents are pitched still closer,
   For we're one day nearer home.—*Cho.*

4 "One day nearer," sings the mar'ner,
   As he glides the waters o'er,
   While the light is softly dying
   On his distant native shore;
   Thus the Christian on life's ocean,
   As his life-boat cuts the foam,
   In the evening cries with rapture,
   "I am one day nearer home."—*Cho.*

FREEPORT. L. M.

Words by E. RINEHART.   Music by Asa Hull.

1. With - in Thy house, O Lord, this day, Once more we meet to learn Thy way;
2. Thy mer-cy, Lord, hath crowned our days, And follows us in all our ways;

With rev'rence and with god-ly fear We in Thy tem - ple now ap-pear.
O fill our hearts with Thy true love, And raise our thoughts to things a - bove.

3.
Jesus, dear Friend, on Thee we call,
Thou art our strength, our all in all;
O let us now Thy presence feel,
While at the mercy-seat we kneel.

DOXOLOGY.
Praise God, from whom all blessings flow;
Praise Him, all creatures here below;
Praise Him above, ye heavenly host;
Praise Father, Son, and Holy Ghost.

Copyright, 1879, *by* Asa Hull.

THE HEAVENLY VISITOR.

Words by Arthur C. Coxe.

Music by Asa Hull.

Words revised by A. C. Hulse.   Music by W. J. Kirkpatrick.

1. Christ is knock-ing, ev - er knocking, At the heart's thrice-bolted door;
2. He is call-ing, ev - er call-ing, In a sad but gen - tle tone;
3. He's en - treat-ing, still en - treat-ing, By His mer - cy, by His care;

Which we're locking, ev - er lock-ing, As we oft have done be - fore.
He would keep thy feet from fall-ing, Cleanse and make thee all His own.
He is knocking and re - peat-ing, Seek-ing for an en-trance there.

Though we hear it, yet we heed not, And still stron-ger bar the door;
Why not an-swer mer - cy's summons, Ere the Spir - it - voice has flown?
Let Him en - ter, let Him en - ter, O - pen wide thy sin-locked door.

CHORUS. *Rep. ad lib.*

Hear it, mortals, o - pen quickly, Christ is waiting, waiting at the door.

CONCLUSION OF **THE HEAVENLY VISITOR,** OPPOSITE PAGE.

2.
Death comes down with ruthless footstep
  To the hall and hut—
Think you death will stand there knocking
  When thy door is shut?
Jesus waiteth, waiteth, waiteth,
  But thy door is fast;
Grieved, away the Saviour turneth,
  Death breaks in the door at last.

3.
Then 'tis time to stand entreating
  Christ to let thee in;
At the gate of heaven beating,
  Wailing for thy sin.
Nay, alas! thou foolish creature,
  Can it be forgot?
Jesus waited long to know thee,
  But He then will know thee not.

ONLY REMEMBERED.

Words by Dr. H. Bonar.
Music by Asa Hull.

1. Up and a-way, like the dew of the morn-ing, Soar - ing from earth to its
2. Shall I be missed if an-oth-er suc-ceed me, Reap-ing the fields I in

Rall. ad lib. .... *a tempo.*

home in the sun ; Thus would I pass from the earth and its toil - ing,
spring-time have sown ? No, for the sow - er may pass from his la - bors,

CHORUS.

On - ly remembered by what I have done, On-ly remembered, on-ly remembered,
On - ly remembered by what he has done.

Only remembered by what I have done, Only remembered by what I have done.

3 Only the truth that in life I have spoken,
   Only the seed that on earth I have shown,
   These shall pass onward when I am forgotten,
   Fruits of the harvest, and what I have done.—*Chorus.*

4 O, when the Saviour shall make up His jewels,
   When the bright crowns of rejoicing are won,
   Then will His faithful and weary disciples
   All be remembered for what they have done.
Chorus. Only remembered, only remembered,
   Only remembered by what they have done.

Words and Music by W. J. Kirkpatrick.

1. There's a firm shelt'ring Rock, and a strong fortress tow'r, Where the weary and
2. 'Tis a ref-uge and rest thro' the con-flicts of life, 'Tis a balm to the

weak can re-new fail-ing pow'r, Where the tempted and care-laden spirit may fly,—
soul, when dismayed in the strife; 'Tis a spring of salvation, a stream nev-er dry,

CHORUS.

O lead me to the Rock that is high-er than I. Lead me to the Rock,
A nev-er failing Rock that is high-er than I. Lead, O, lead me to the Rock, O lead me,

Lead me to the Rock, Lead me to the Rock that is higher than I.
Lead, O, lead me to the Rock, O lead me,

3 'Tis my comfort and stay, my deliv'rer and joy,
When the heart is o'erwhelmed with the ills that annoy ;
When the fierce sweeping tempest of sorrow is nigh,
O, lead me to the Rock that is higher than I.—*Chorus.*

4 When the few joys of life are all flitting away,
Like the soft fading light at the closing of day,
When the shadow of death steals the light from my eye,
O, lead me to the Rock that is higher than I.—*Chorus.*

THE ANGEL AT THE PORTAL.

Allegretto sostenuto.

Words and Music by Asa Hull.

1. I fear not the gloom of mid-night, I dread not the storm at sea;
   I fear not, O, I fear not, Nor heed darksome waves of sin;

My Saviour can calm the raging billows, And il-lu-mine a path for me.
For the An-gel is waiting at the por-tal Of glo-ry to let me in.

CHORUS.

Wait-ing, wait-ing, wait-ing, wait-ing, wait-ing to let me in; For the
An-gel is wait-ing at the por-tal, Is wait-ing to let me in.

2.
I heed not the world's allurements,
  While glory's bright star I see ;
I'll steer for the bright and shining portal,
  That the angel will ope for me.
I'm seeking for joys immortal,
  And crowns that the righteous win ;—
And the angel is waiting at the portal
  Of glory to let me in.—*Chorus.*

3.
I shrink not from cross or trial,
  I shun not the narrow way ;
I'll watch at the ever-op'ning portal
  For a glimpse of eternal day.
I'll join in the praise eternal,
  And here will my song begin ;
For the angel is waiting at the portal
  Of glory to let me in.—*Chorus.*

Words by Rev. A. A. GRALEY.   Music by W. A. CORNELL. Arr'd.

1. Je-sus sought and saved me, When a wand'ring child ; In the fountain laved me,

Wretched and de - filed.   Dried the eyes so tear - ful, Bade the anguish cease,

CHORUS.

And the heart so fearful, Filled with heav'nly peace.   All my song shall be,....
shall be,

" Je - sus died for me,"   Never sweeter song was sung, Than "Jesus died for me."
for me,

2 All unclean He found me,
   Poor and comfortless ;
   But He threw around me
   Robes of righteousness ;
   Hushed the cry of sadness,
   Taught me to rejoice,
   And to songs of gladness
   Tuned my heart and voice,
     Chorus.—All my song, etc.

3 Saviour, Thine forever
   I would wholly be ;
   Let me never, never,
   Tire of serving Thee.
   Gazing on Thy beauty
   Will my time employ ;
   Toil is more than duty,
   'Tis my brightest joy.
     Chorus—All my song, etc.

WHEN THE MISTS HAVE CLEARED AWAY.

Words arranged for this work.

Music by S. J. Vail.

1. When the mists have roll'd in splen-dor From the beau-ty of the hills,
2. If we err in hu-man blindness, And for-get that we are dust;

And the sun-shine warm and ten-der, Falls in beau-ty on the rills,
If we miss the law of kind-ness, When we strug-gle to be just:

We may read love's shin-ing let-ter In the rain-bow of the spray:
Snow-y wings of peace shall cov-er All the pain that clouds our day,

We shall know each oth-er bet-ter, When the mists have clear'd a-way.
When the wea-ry watch is o-ver, And the mists have clear'd a-way.

CHORUS.

We shall know as we are known, Nev-er more to walk a-lone,

In the dawn-ing of the morn - ing, When the mists have clear'd a - way.

3 When the mists shall rise above us
  As our Father knows His own,
Face to face with those that love us,
  We shall know as we are known.

Just beyond the darkened shadows
  Floats the golden fringe of day;
We shall see its wondrous brightness,
  When the mists have clear'd away.

THE CHRISTIAN HERO.

With energy.   Words and Music by Rev. E. H. NEVIN, D.D.

1. Live on the field of bat - tle!   Be ear - nest in the fight;
2. Watch on the field of bat - tle!   The foe is ev - 'ry - where,

Stand forth with man-ly cour - age,   And strug - gle for the right.
His fi - ery darts fly thick - ly,   Like light - ning, thro' the air.

Live,   live,   live! Live on the field of bat - tle.
Watch, watch, watch! Watch on the field of bat - tle.

3 Pray on the field of battle!
  God works with those who pray;
His mighty arm can nerve us,
  And make us win the day.
Pray, pray, pray!
Pray on the field of battle.

4 Die on the field of battle!
  'Tis noble thus to die;
God smiles on valiant soldiers,—
  Their record is on high!
Die, die, die!
Die on the field of battle.

NEW WHITER THAN SNOW.

Allegretto. (New Arrangement.)   Words and Music by Asa Hull.

1. Dear Sav-iour, how oft-en my heart has been sad, How oft-en it
2. O help me, dear Sav-iour, to pa-tient-ly wait Thy com-ing and

murmurs, when it should be glad ; Come, reign in this bosom, cast out ev-'ry foe,
cleansing, a-new to cre-ate ; The grace of full par-don, O wilt Thou bestow,

CHORUS.

And wash me that I may be whit-er than snow. Whit-er than snow, yes,
And wash me that I may be whit-er than snow.

whit-er than snow, O wash me that I may be whit-er than snow.

3 My time and my talents, my goods I resign
 To Thee, my dear Saviour, they always were Thine ;
 O make me Thy steward in all things below,
 And wash me that I may be whiter than snow.—*Chorus.*

4 My dwelling though pitched in a wilderness here,
 To me will be Eden, if Thou, Lord, art near ;
 Thy presence is life everlasting, I know,
 Thy blood, it hath cleansed me, I'm whiter than snow.—*Chorus.*

Copyright, 1877, by Asa Hull.

SOLO OR DUET.   WEBBE.

1. Come, ye dis - con - so - late, wher - e'er ye lan - guish; Come, at the
2. Joy of the des - o - late, light of the stray - ing, Hope of the
3. Here see the Bread of Life; see wa - ters flow - ing Forth from the

DUET, 1st *time.* Rep. FULL CHORUS.

mer - cy - seat fer - vent - ly kneel; Here bring your wounded hearts,
pen - i - tent, fade - less and pure; Here speaks the Com - fort - er,
throne of God, pure from a - bove; Come to the feast of love;

here tell your an - guish, Earth has no sorrow that Heav'n cannot heal.
ten - der - ly say - ing; Earth has no sorrow that Heav'n cannot cure.
come, ev - er know-ing, Earth has no sorrow but Heav'n can remove.

SECOND HYMN FOR **NEW WHITER THAN SNOW,** OPPOSITE PAGE.

1 DEAR Jesus, I long to be perfectly whole;
I want Thee forever to live in my soul;
Break down every idol, cast out every foe;
Now wash me, and I shall be whiter than snow.—*Chorus.*

2 Dear Jesus, let nothing unholy remain;
Apply Thine own blood, and extract every stain;
To get this blest washing, I all things forego;
Now wash me, and I shall be whiter than snow.—*Chorus.*

3 Dear Jesus, thou see'st I patiently wait;
Come now, and within me a new heart create;
To those who have sought Thee, Thou never saidst no,—
Now wash me, and I shall be whiter than snow.—*Chorus.*

4 Dear Jesus, for this I most humbly entreat;
I wait, blessed Lord, at Thy crucified feet;
By faith, for my cleansing, I see Thy blood flow,—
Now wash me, and I shall be whiter than snow.—*Chorus.*

JAMES NICHOLSON.

THE SUMMER TIME.

Words by W. H. FLAVILLE.

Music by ASA HULL.

1. O come un-to the Saviour, for why will you delay ? The Spir-it now in-
2. O come un-to the Saviour, He's mer-ci-ful and true, A full and free sal-

vites you, O do not turn a-way ; The door is o-pen now, but it
va-tion, He kind-ly of-fers you ; O come while yet you may, or you'll

will be closed at last, For the sum-mer will be end-ed, and the
find it true at last That the sum-mer time is end-ed, and the

CHORUS.

har-vest will be past. O come, sinner, come ! for thy sands are running fast ;
har-vest time is past.

Soon the sum-mer will be end-ed, and the har-vest will be past.

Copyright, 1877, by ASA HULL.

Words by Rev. M. L. Hofford.　　　　　　Music by J. H. Rosecrans.

1. Je - ru - sa - lem, the beau - ti - ful! Its glo - ries are un - told;
2. Je - ru - sa - lem, the beau - ti - ful! Its gates of pearl - y white,
3. Je - ru - sa - lem, the beau - ti - ful! My ev - er - last - ing rest!

Its walls are built of pre-cious stones, Its pavements made of gold;
To voice of prayer and song of praise, Are o - pen day and night;
My glo - rious home, the saints' a- bode, The cit - y of the blest;

Its mansions for the ransomed ones In matchless splendor shine;
And shin - ing ones a - round the throne In sweet - er rap - ture sing ;—
The tem - ple of the Ho - ly One, Thy light is all di - vine;

Je - ru - sa - lem, the beau - ti - ful! Je - ru - sa - lem di - vine!
Je - ru - sa - lem, the beau - ti - ful! Where saints their tribute bring.
Je - ru - sa - lem, the beau - ti - ful! I love to call thee mine.

Copyright, 1879, by Asa Hull.

CONCLUSION OF **THE SUMMER TIME,** OPPOSITE PAGE.

3 O come unto the Saviour, the night is coming on,
　There's danger in delaying, for the Spirit may be gone ;
　He's waiting to release you from the chains that sin has cast,
　Ere the summer time is ended, and the harvest time is past.—*Chorus.*

4 O come unto the Saviour, nor let Him plead in vain,
　There is a crown of glory, and eternal life to gain ;
　His offers now accept, ere the sky is overcast,
　Or the summer time is ended, and the harvest time is past.—*Chorus.*

THE VOICE OF LOVE.

Words by J. L. LOUDERBACK.   Music by W. J. KIRKPATRICK.

1. Wea - ry, wand'ring child of grief, Hear the Sav-iour's plead-ing call,
2. What tho' steeped in dark-est crime, Foul, un-clean, and stain'd with sin,

Who for sin - ners, e'en the chief, Died to save you from the fall.
Je - sus knows it all the time, Seeks to make and keep you clean.

CHORUS.

O believe Him, O receive Him, Christ in mercy bids you come ;........
bids you come ;

O believe Him, O re-ceive Him,—In thy sins no lon-ger roam.

3 In thy course, O wand'rer, pause,
  Listen to the voice of love,—
Christ the Saviour pleads thy cause
In the courts of heaven above.
  Chorus.—O believe Him, etc.

4 And when life's great race is run,
  And thy conflicts all are past ;
Heav'n in view, thy victory won,
God shall crown you His at last.
  Chorus—O believe Him, etc.

Words by W. H. BELLAMY.   Music by J. P. TRUITT.

1. The home where changes nev-er come, Nor pain, nor sor-row, toil, nor care;
2. Yet, when bow'd down beneath the load By heav'n ordain'd thine earthly lot,

Yes! 'tis a bright and bless-ed home; Who would not fain be rest-ing there?
Thou yearn'st to reach that blest a-bode; Wait, meek-ly wait, and murmur not.

CHORUS.

Wait, meek-ly wait, and mur-mur not, and murmur not, and mur-mur not;

Wait, meek-ly wait, and mur-mur not, O, wait, and mur-mur not.

3 If in thy path some thorns are found,
   Oh, think who bore them on His brow;
  If grief thy sorrowing heart has found,
   They reached a holier than thou.—*Chorus.*

4 Toil on, nor deem, though sore it be,
   One sigh unheard, one prayer forgot;
  The day of rest will dawn for thee:
   Wait, meekly wait, and murmur not.—*Chorus.*

STAND UP FOR JESUS.

Words by R. Torrey.   Music by Asa Hull.

1. Stand up for Je - sus, Christian, stand, Firm as a rock on ocean's strand!
2. Stand up for Je - sus, Christian, stand ! Sound forth His name o'er sea and land !

Beat back the waves of sin that roll, Like rag - ing floods, around thy soul !
Spread ye His glo-rious word a - broad, Till all the world shall own Him Lord.

CHORUS.   *Rit ad lib.*

Stand up for Je - sus, no - bly stand, Firm as a rock on o-cean's strand !

A tempo.

Stand up His righteous cause de - fend ; Stand up for Je - sus your best friend,

3.
Stand up for Jesus, Christian, stand !
Lift high the cross with steadfast hand,
Till heathen lands, with wond'ring eye,
Its rising glory shall descry.
   Chorus.—Stand up for Jesus, etc.

4.
Stand up for Jesus, Christian, stand !
Soon with the blest immortal band
We'll dwell for aye, life's journey o'er,
In realms of light, on heav'n's bright shore.
   Chorus.—Stand up for Jesus, etc.

Words by Mrs E. W. Chapman.   Music by J. H. Tenney.

1. A bea - con bright the Christian stands Up - on the shore of time;
2. A tow - er high the Christian stands, A clear and shin - ing light,
3. Grand sen - ti - nel up - on life's coast, Be faith-ful, true, and brave;

A light-house built on sol - id rock, That rears its head sub - lime.
To cast a gleam a - cross the sea Of earth's dark, gloomy night.
And ev - er keep your light a - blaze, Be - night - ed souls to save.

CHORUS.

Look !   Look !   Look to the light-house,
Look to the light - house, Look to the light - house,

sai - lor, It tells of danger near ; Look ! Look !
Look to the light-house, Look to the light-house,

Look to the light - house, sai - lor, And guide thy ves - sel clear.

TRUSTING THE LORD.

Words by E. RINEHART.

Music by ASA HULL.

1. Watching thro' the night and wait-ing for the dawn; Look-ing for the first bright ray of morn; Feel-ing all the gloom of the mid - night hour, Yet I'm trust-ing all to His love and pow'r.

2. Liv - ing in the val - ley, hum-ble, meek, and low; Thus it is I triumph o'er ev - 'ry foe; Wait-ing till the sum-mons shall call me home; Out in - to the sunshine be - yond the gloom.

3. Work-ing for the Mas - ter, pa - tient-ly I wait; Knock-ing for ad - mittance at Mer - c'ys gate; Trust-ing Him to guide, where I can - not see; Knowing that His care is still o - ver me.

CHORUS.

Watching thro' the night; Wait-ing for the dawn; Look - ing for the
Watch - ing thro' the night; Wait - ing for the dawn;

first bright ray of morn; Feel - ing all the gloom of the
Feel - ing all the gloom of the

mid - night hour, Yet I'm trusting all to His love and pow'r.

JESUS DIED FOR YOU.

Music by S. J. Vail.

1. O, what a - maz - ing words of grace Are in the gos - pel found !
2. Poor, sin - ful, thirst - y faint - ing souls, Are free - ly wel - come here ;

Suit - ed to ev - 'ry sin - ner's case Who knows the joy - ful sound.
Sal - va - tion like a riv - er rolls, A - bun - dant, free, and clear.

CHORUS.

Je - sus died for you, Je - sus died for me ; Yes, Je - sus died for all mankind ;

Bless God, He died for me.

3 Come, then, with all your wants and wounds ;
  Your every burden bring ;
Here love, unchanging love, abounds,—
  A deep, celestial spring.—*Cho.*

4 Millions of sinners vile as you,
  Have here found life and peace ;
Come, then, and prove its virtues too,
  And drink, adore, and bless.—*Cho.*

Music by Asa Hull.

1. An - y-where with Je - sus, says the Christian heart;   Let Him take me
2. An - y-where with Je - sus, tho' He lead - eth   me   Where the path is

where He will, so we do   not   part;   Al - ways sit - ting at His feet, there's
rough and long, where dan-gers   be ;   Tho' He tak - eth from me all   I

no room for fears ;   An - y-where with Je-sus, in this vale of   tears.
love here be - low,   An - y-where with Je-sus, glad-ly will I   go.

CHORUS.

An - y-where with Je - sus,   ev - 'ry-where I   go;   Je - sus shall my

lea - der be, while I   sojourn be - low ;   Al - ways sit-ting at His feet, there's

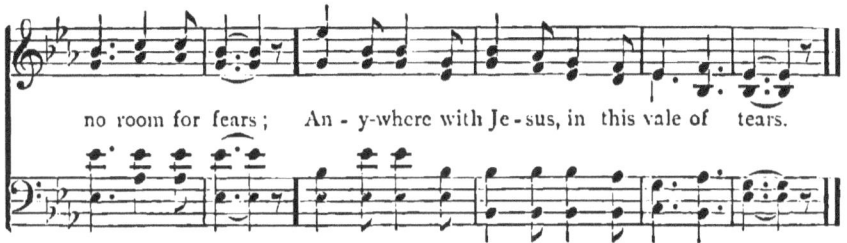

no room for fears; An - y-where with Je - sus, in this vale of tears.

3 Anywhere with Jesus, though it be the tomb,
With its fearful terror, with its dreaded gloom ;
Though it be the weariness of a long-drawn life,
Fainting in the constant toil, drooping in the strife.—*Chorus.*

4 Anywhere with Jesus, for it cannot be,
Dreary, dark, or desolate, where He is with me ;
He will love me alway, ev'ry need He'll supply,
Anywhere with Jesus, should I live or die.—*Chorus.*

ITALIAN HYMN.

Words by C. WESLEY.   Music by GIARDINI.

1. Come, Thou Al - might - y King, Help us Thy name to sing ;
2. Come, Thou In - car - nate Word, Gird on Thy might - y sword,

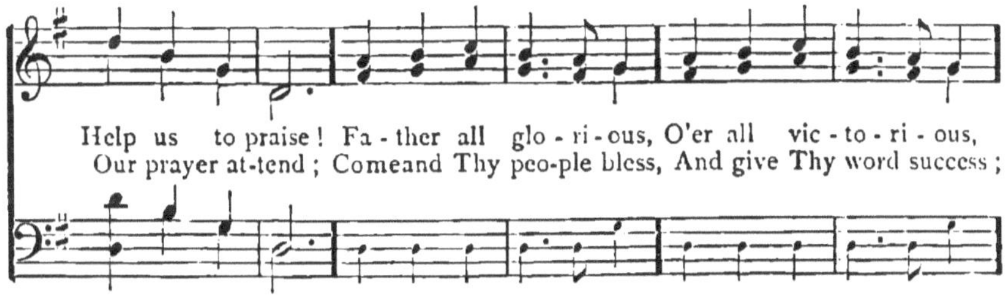

Help us to praise! Fa - ther all glo - ri - ous, O'er all vic - to - ri - ous,
Our prayer at-tend ; Come and Thy peo-ple bless, And give Thy word success ;

Come and reign o - ver us, An-cient of Days.
Spi - rit of ho - li-ness, On us de-scend.

3.
Come, Holy Comforter,
Thy sacred witness bear,
In this glad hour ;
Thou who almighty art,
Now rule in every heart,
And ne'er from us depart,
Spirit of power.

IS IT TRUE?

Words by E. R. LATTA.　　　　　　　　　　　　　Music by J. H. TENNEY.

1. Is it true that in the garden of Geth-sem - a - ne　My Re - deemer wept and
2. Is it true that He the crown of piercing thorns did wear? Is it true that up the
3. Is it true that my Re-deemer loves my spir-it still, And will fit me up a

struggled, wept in pray'r for me? Drops of sweat as blood were fall-ing, death seem'd
mountain He the cross did bear, And was cru - ci - fied up - on it, thus to
man-sion, if I on - ly will? O my heart, make haste to serve Him, while on

draw - ing nigh; Sav - iour, was it for the sake of sin - ners such as I?
ran - som me? O a - maz - ing love and mer - cy! Sav-iour, can it be?
earth I dwell, That in death my voice can whis-per, whis-per it is well!

CHORUS.

Is it true,　　　　　　　is it true　　　　　　Thou such
Is it true, O pre-cious Sav-iour? Is it true, O pre-cious Sav - iour? Is it

love　　　hast　　　shown? Come and make us, blessed Sav - iour, ev - er -
true that Thou such love has shown?

more Thine own ! Bless-ed Sav - - iour, ev - er - more Thine own !
Come and make us, bless - ed Sav-iour,

FREDERICK 11s.

Words by W. A. MOHLENBERG.   Music by G. KINGSLEY.

1. I would not live al - way ; I ask not to stay, Where storm af-ter
2. I would not live al - way ; no ! wel - come the tomb, Since Je - sus has

storm ris - es dark o'er the way ; The few lu - cid mornings that
lain there, I dread not its gloom ; There, sweet be my rest, till He

dawn on us here, Are enough for life's woes, full e - nough for its cheer.
bid me a - rise, To hail Him in tri - umph de - scend-ing the skies.

3 Who, who would live alway away from his God,
Away from yon heaven, that blissful abode,
Where the rivers of pleasure flow o'er the bright plains,
And the noontide of glory eternally reigns.

4 There the saints of all ages in harmony meet ;
Their Saviour and brethren transported to greet ;
While the anthems of rapture unceasingly roll,
And the smile of the Lord is the feast of the soul.

I'M NEARING HOME.

Words by MARY D. JAMES.　　　　　　　　Music by ASA HULL.

1. I'm near-ing home ! Life's wintry blast Will soon be o'er, its gloom be past ;
2. Tho' rocks and quicksands in-ter-vene, And rag - ing bil - lows roll between,

O, I shall gain the port at last :—I'm near-ing, near-ing home !
My Pi - lot's skill will bring me in :—I'm near-ing, near-ing home !

REFRAIN.

Near - - - ing home !.... Near - - - ing home !....
Near-ing my beau-ti - ful, beau - ti - ful home, Near-ing my beau-ti - ful heaven - ly home.

O, I shall gain the port at last :—I'm near - ing, nearing my home !
My Pi - lot's skill will bring me in :—I'm near - ing, nearing my home !

3　These heavy gales do me no harm :
　　Terrific storms do not alarm ;
　　My spirit rests in sweetest calm :—
　　　I'm nearing, nearing home !
　　Nearing home, nearing home !
　　My spirit rests in sweetest calm :—
　　　I'm nearing, nearing my home !

4　O home, sweet home! I'll soon be there,
　　The bliss of the redeemed to share ;
　　Only a few more storms to bear :—
　　　I'm nearing, nearing home !
　　Nearing home, nearing home !
　　Only a few more storms to bear :—
　　　I'm nearing, nearing my home !

Moderato, con Espressione.

Music by Asa Hull.

1. On - ly wait - ing till the shad - ows Are a lit - tle long - er grown;
2. On - ly wait - ing till the an - gels O - pen wide the mys - tic gate;
3. On - ly wait - ing till the reap - ers Have the last sheaf gathered home;

On - ly wait - ing till the glim - mer Of the day's last beams are flown;
At the por - tals long I've wait - ed, Wea - ry, poor and des - o - late;
For the sum - mer time is fad - ed, And the au - tumn leaves have come;

Till the light of earth is fad - ed From the heart once full of day;
E - ven now I hear their foot - steps And their voi - ces far a - way;
Quick-ly, reap - ers! quick-ly gath - er The last ripe hours of my heart;

Till the stars of heav'n are break-ing Thro' the twi - light soft and gray;
If they call me I am wait - ing, On - ly wait - ing to o - bey;
For the bloom of life is withered, And I'm read - y to de - part;

Rit. ad lib.

Break - ing, break - ing Thro' the twi - light soft and gray,
Wait - ing, wait - ing, On - ly wait - ing to o - bey.
Read - y, read - y, I am read - y to de - part.

OPEN WIDE THE DOOR.

Words by Mrs. C. L. SCHACKLOCK.　　　Music by T. FRANK ALLEN.

1. We are com - ing, we are com - ing From the dark-some ways of sin,
2. On - ly thro' Thy ten - der mer - cy Can we hope to en - ter there,

And we seek the heav'n-ly king - dom, Je - sus, Sav - iour, let me in!
Where the streams of life is flow - ing, Where the flow'rs are ev - er fair.

From the fold, O gen - tle Shep-herd! We would wan - der nev - er more;
In that home, O bless-ed Sav - iour! When this earth - ly life is o'er,

To Thy lov - ing breast en - fold us, O - pen wide for us the door.
We would dwell with Thee for-ev - er; O - pen wide for us the door.

CHORUS.

O - pen wide for us the door! We will leave Thee nev - er - more;

To Thy lov-ing breast en-fold us, O-pen wide for us the door.

WORK, WORK FOR GOD.

Words by Eliza J. Coffin.   Music by Asa Hull.

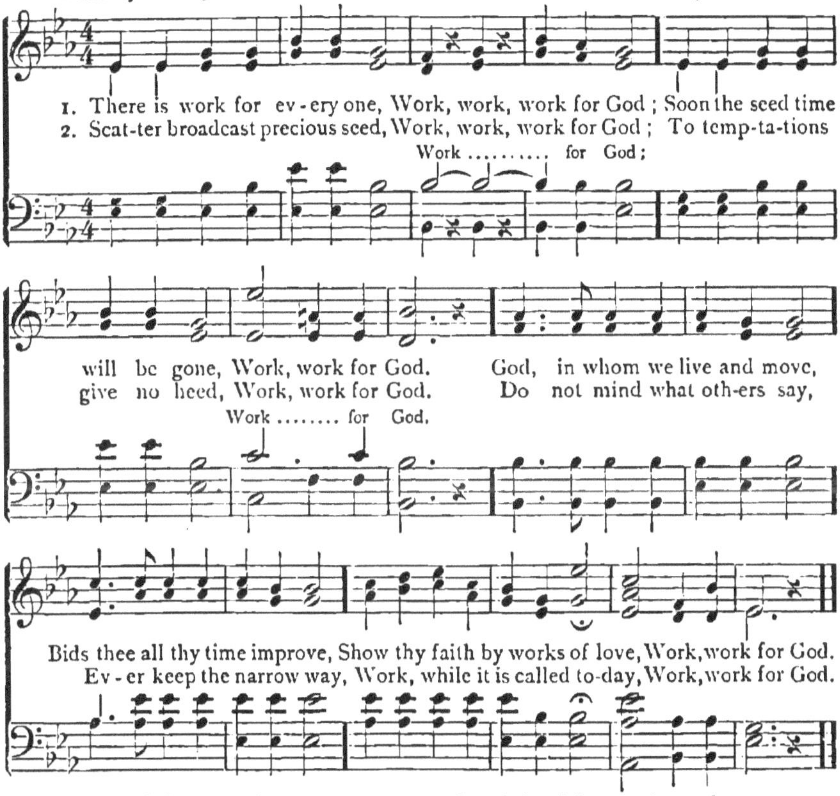

1. There is work for ev-ery one, Work, work, work for God ; Soon the seed time
2. Scat-ter broadcast precious seed, Work, work, work for God ; To temp-ta-tions

Work .... for God ;

will be gone, Work, work for God.   God, in whom we live and move,
give no heed, Work, work for God.   Do not mind what oth-ers say,

Work .... for God.

Bids thee all thy time improve, Show thy faith by works of love, Work, work for God.
Ev - er keep the narrow way, Work, while it is called to-day, Work, work for God.

3 Be thyself first pure in heart,
Work, work, work for God ;
Then thy joy to all impart,
Work, work for God.
Tell the story of the cross,
Counting earthly things but dross,
Thou shalt never suffer loss,
Work, work for God.

4 Laud the right, condemn the wrong,
Work, work, work for God ;
All results to Him belong,
Work, work for God ;
Find thy joy in God's sweet will,
Every promise He'll fulfill,
And His peace will keep thee still,
Work, work for God.

Words by D. D. Buck, D.D.   Music by Asa Hull.

1. If we can not plant our cot-tage 'Mid an E-den's blooming bow'rs,
2. If we can not win a ti-tle To enwreathe our humble name;

Whil-ing life's de-light-ful sum-mer Gai-ly 'mid un-fading flow'rs—
If we boast not birth nor beau-ty, Wealth nor wis-dom, might nor fame—

We with ho-ly love can la-bor, Till-ing Zi-on's fer-tile lands;
We can still be kind-ly-heart-ed, Act-ing well our low-ly part;

We can con-se-crate to du-ty Will-ing hearts and read-y hands.
And, tho' men may be un-grate-ful, God will prize the hum-ble heart.

3 If we can not read the future,
    Whether weal or woe betide,
If within the veil of darkness
    Mercy from our vision hide,—
We can understand our mission,
    What is here to do or bear ;
We can love and help each other,
    And the cross with Jesus share.

4 Let us, then, be ever doing ;
    Day declineth, night is near ;
Short the time of toil and suff'ring ;
    Jesus numbers every tear.
See ! the pearly gates are opening ;
    Lo ! the splendor from above ;
List to lov'd ones yonder singing,
    Welcome to the land of love.

Words by ELIZA J. COFFIN.   Music by J. H. ROSECRANS.

1. Dear Sav - iour, does Thy love, So won - der - ful and free,
2. Give us a deep - er love, That loves Thy love a - lone;

De - light to own Thy weak-est child, Who up - ward looks to Thee?
Re - signs all hope of earth - ly gain, This wondrous gift to own.

CHORUS.

O love! O won - drous love! O love that stoops to me!

Slower.

A love that cov - ers all my sins, And makes me free to Thee.

3 Thee only would we love ;
  Be this our constant aim,
To lose all thought of self in Thee,
And glorify Thy name.
    Chorus.—O love, etc.

4 Then beautify us, Lord,
  And may we meekly show
Our hearts to be Thy temple-home,
Where love shall ever flow.
    Chorus.—O love, etc.

O COME, COME TO-DAY.

Words by E. RINEHART.　　　　　　　　　　　　　　　Music by ASA HULL.

1. Burden'd soul, come seek the Saviour, Hear Him call, "Come un-to Me;"
2. Look not at thy guilt or sta - tion, Tho' un - wor - thy, He'll re-ceive;

In His sight find grace and fa - vor, In His love there's rest for thee.
Je - sus died for thy sal - va - tion, Waits to bring thee thy re-prieve.

CHORUS,

Then come,　　　come a-way,　　　The Sav-iour calls, why lon-ger wait?
Then come, come a-way, O　come, come a-way,

O come,　　　come to-day,　　　For the morrow may be too late, may
O come, come to-day, O　come, come to-day;

pp

be too late, may be too late.

3 Full salvation Jesus offers ;
　Full redemption in His blood ;
Come, accept the proffered pardon,
　And be reconciled to God.

4 Will you come ? while He is pleading !
　Will you come and be at rest ?
Follow now the Spirit's leading,
　Come, for 'tis your Lord's request.

By permission.

Music by T. J. COOK.

1. Beau-ti-ful Zi - on, built a - bove, Beau-ti-ful cit - y that I love!
2. Beau-ti-ful heav'n where all is light, Beau-ti-ful angels, cloth'd in white;

Beau-ti-ful gates of pear-ly white, Beau-ti-ful tem-ple—God its light!
Beau-ti-ful strains that nev-er tire, Beau-ti-ful harps thro' all the choir;

He who was slain on Cal-va-ry, O-pens those pear-ly
There shall I join the cho-rus sweet, Wor-ship-ing at the

CHORUS.

gates to me. Zi - on, Zi-on, love-ly Zi-on, Beau-ti-ful
Sav-iour's feet.

Rep. pp ad lib.

Zi - on, cit-ty of our God.

3 Beautiful crowns on every brow,
Beautiful palms the conquerors show;
Beautiful robes the ransomed wear,
Beautiful all who enter there;
Thither I press with eager feet,
There shall my rest be long and sweet.

Cho.—Zion, Zion, lovely Zion,
Beautiful Zion, city of our God.

By permission.   Music by WM. G. FISHER.

1. I love to tell the sto - ry : Of un - seen things a-bove, Of Je - sus
2. I love to tell the sto - ry : More won-der-ful it seems, Than all the

and His glo - ry, Of Je - sus and His love. I love to tell the
gold - en fan - cies Of all our gold-en dreams. I love to tell the

sto - ry, Be - cause I know it's true; It sat - is - fies my long-ings, As
sto - ry : It did so much for me! And that is just the rea - son I

CHORUS.

noth - ing else would do. I love to tell the sto - ry, 'Twill be my theme in
tell it now to thee.

glo - ry, To tell the old, old sto - ry Of Je - sus and His love.

Words by Rev. E. A. HOFFMAN.   Music by ASA HULL. From "Songs of Faith."

1, I am com-ing to the Saviour, At His feet I bow; I am pleading for His
2. All my sin and guilt confessing, At His feet I bow; I am wait-ing for His
3. In con-trition humbly kneeling, At His feet I bow; I am seeking grace and

CHORUS.

fa - vor, Just now, just now. I am com-ing, I am com-ing, I am
bless - ing, Just now, just now.
heal - ing, Just now, just now.

com - ing just now, I am com-ing, I am com-ing, I am com-ing just now.

4 I believe Him, I believe Him,
   At His feet I bow;
I receive Him, I receive Him,
Just now, just now.—*Chorus.*

5 Hallelujah! Hallelujah!
   To the Lamb once slain;
Hallelujah! Hallelujah!
Amen! Amen!—*Chorus.*

CONCLUSION OF **I LOVE TO TELL THE STORY,** OPPOSITE PAGE.

3 I love to tell the story:
   'Tis pleasant to repeat
What seems, each time I tell it,
   More wonderfully sweet.
I love to tell the story:
   For some have never heard
The Message of salvation
   From God's own holy word.—*Cho.*

4 I love to tell the story:
   For those who know it best
Seem hungering and thirsting
   To hear it like the rest.
And when, in scenes of glory,
   I sing the NEW, NEW SONG,
Twill be—the OLD, OLD STORY
   That I have loved so long.—*Cho.*

UNDER HIS WINGS.

Words by James Nicholson.　　　　　　　　　　　　Music by Asa Hull.

1. In God I have found a re-treat, Where I can se-cure-ly a-bide;
2. I dread not the ter-ror by night; No ar-row can harm me by day;
3. The pes-ti-lence walk-ing a-bout, When darkness has set-tled a-broad,

No ref-uge nor rest so complete, And here I in-tend to re-side.
His shad-ow has cover-ed me quite; My fears He has driv-en a-way.
Can nev-er com-pel me to doubt The presence and pow-er of God.

CHORUS.

O, what com-fort it brings, as my soul sweet-ly sings:

I am safe from all dan-ger while un-der His wings.

4 The wasting destruction at noon,
　　No fearful forboding can bring ;
With Jesus, my soul doth commune,
　　His perfect salvation I sing.—*Cho.*

5 A thousand may fall at my side,
　　Ten thousand fall at my right hand ;
Above me His wings are spread wide,
　　Beneath them in safety I stand.—*Cho.*

FOR YOU AND ME.

Words by Mrs E. C. Ellsworth.   Music by J. H. Tenney.

1. There is a mansion bright and fair, For you and me ; There is a welcome
2. There is a garment clear as light, For you and me ; There is a robe of
3. There is a ta - ble rich-ly spread For you and me ; There is a full sup-

wait - ing there For you   and   me : Why home-less then, and wand'ring wide,
pur - est white For you   and   me : O why on rags a thought be-stow,
ply of bread For you   and   me : Then why in want and sore dis - tress,

Since Je - sus doth a place provide, For you, O sin - ner, you and me.
Since Christ hath raiment white as snow, For you, O sin - ner, you and me.
Since Je - sus doth all things pos-sess, For you, O sin - ner, you and me.

REFRAIN. *Rep. pp ad lib.*

For you   and   me,   For you, yes, you and me ; For
For you   and me,   For you and me ;

Ritard.

you   and   me,   For you, yes, you and me.
For you   and   me,

SING OF HIS LOVE.

Music by W. J. KIRKPATRICK.

1. Chil-dren of the heav'nly King, As ye jour-ney sweet-ly sing,
2. We are trav-'ling home to God, In the way our fathers trod;

Sing your Saviour's worth-y praise, Glo-rious in His works and ways.
They are hap-py now, and we Soon their hap-pi-ness shall see.

CHORUS.

Sing of His love, ye angels of light; Carol His praise, ye seraphs so
Sing of His love, ye an-gels of light; Car-ol His praise, ye

bright; Join in the song, ye saints, with delight ; Praising the
seraphs so bright ; Join in the song, ye saints, with delight ;

Rit. ad lib.

name, won-der-ful name of Je - sus.

3 Fear not, brethren, joyful stand,
On the borders of our land ;
Jesus Christ, our Father's Son,
Bids us undismayed go on.

4 Lord, obediently we'll go,
Gladly leaving all below ;
Only Thou our leader be,
And we still will follow Thee.

Words by Rev. JOHN PARKER.   Music by ASA HULL.

1. More Thou art than friend or broth-er, Thou art all to me;
2. Glad to bring my con - se - cra - tion, Give my life to Thee;

Not in earth or heav'n an-oth-er Half so dear as Thee.
Glad to know Thy full sal - va - tion, Ho - li - er to be.

CHORUS.

All in all, O Christ, Thou art, Thou dost fill my trust - ing heart;

All in all, O Christ, Thou art, Thou dost fill my trust - ing heart.

3.
Thou hast washed my soul with whiteness,
I have liberty ;
Thou dost fill my life with brightness,
And sincerity.
Chorus.—All in all, O Christ, etc.

4.
Henceforth Thou my perfect Saviour,
All in all to me ;
Walking ever in Thy favor
I Thy face shall see.
Chorus.—All in all, O Christ, etc.

Copyright, 1874, by ASA HULL.

MERCY'S GATE.

Words by SAMUEL CALLAN.

Music by ASA HULL.

1. There are joys we fondly cher - ish, While we tread this vale of earth ;
   All who share the bliss of heav-en En - ter'd in at mer-cy's gate ;

There are those that never per - ish, But in heav'n they have their birth.
Thro' the grace by Je - sus giv - en, They have reach'd their high estate.

CHORUS.

Let us ev - er strive to en - - - ter, Nev-er for the morrow wait ;
Let us strive to en - ter, Nev-er for the mor-row wait ;

Strive to en-ter, strive to en-ter, En-ter in at mercy's gate............
Ritard.
at mercy's gate.

2 Earth may have its many pleasures,
    They are fleeting as a day ;
But above are dearer treasures,
    That shall never pass away.
In the path of right and duty
    Many ills may be our fate ;
But religion has a beauty ;
    It is found at mercy's gate.

3 Up the hill ascending ever,
    With our eyes upon the goal,
Let the world's allurements never
    Cause us to forget the soul.
Soon our toil will here be ended,
    Bright rewards for us await,
When to Him we are ascended,
    Who has opened mercy's gate.

Words by E. M. HALL.   Music by J. T. GRAPE. Arr. by ASA HULL.

1. I hear the Sav-iour say, Thy strength in-deed is small,
2. Lord, now in-deed I find Thy blood, and Thine a-lone,

Child of weak-ness, watch and pray, Find in me Thy all in all.
Can change the lep-er's spots, And melt the heart of stone.

CHORUS.

Je - sus paid it all; All to Him I owe;

Sin had left a crim-son stain, He wash'd it white as snow.

3 For nothing good have I,
　Whereby Thy grace to claim,
I'll wash my garments white
In the blood of Calvary's Lamb.

4 And then complete in Him,
　My robe His righteousness,
Close-shelter'd 'neath His side,
1 am divinely blest.

5 When from my dying bed
　My ransom'd soul shall rise,
Then " Jesus paid it all!"
Shall fill the vaulted skies.

6 And when before the throne
　I stand, in Him complete,
I'll lay my trophies down,
All down at Jesus' feet.

Moderato.

From RINK.

1.
{ There is   a land   of pure   de-light, Where saints immor-tal reign ;
{ In-fi-nite   day   ex-cludes the night, And pleas-ures ban-ish pain ;

There ev-er-last-ing spring a-bides, And nev-er with-'ring flowr's;

Death, like   a   nar-row   sea, di-vides This heav'n-ly land from ours.

2.

Sweet fields, beyond the swelling flood,
    Stand dressed in living green ;
So, to the Jews, old Canaan stood,
    While Jordan rolled between :
But tim'rous mortals start, and shrink
    To cross this narrow sea,
And linger, shiv'ring, on the brink,
    And fear to launch away.

3.

Oh, could we make our doubts remove,
    Those gloomy doubts that rise,
And see the Canaan that we love
    With unbeclouded eyes,—
Could we but climb where Moses stood,
    And view the landscape o'er,
Not Jordan's stream, nor death's cold flood,
    Should fright us from the shore.

SONGS OF THE CROSS.

Words by Mrs. E. C. ELLSWORTH.

Music by J. H. TENNEY.

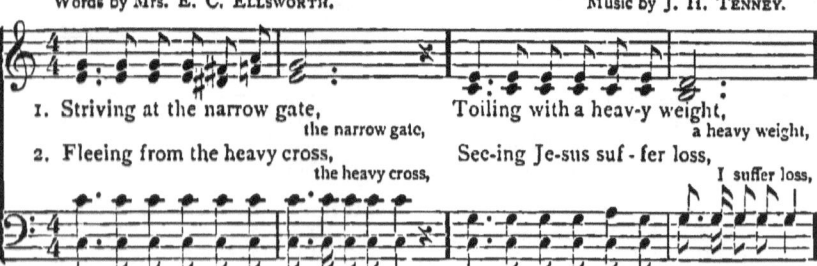

1. Striving at the narrow gate,   Toiling with a heav-y weight,
     the narrow gate,   a heavy weight,
2. Fleeing from the heavy cross,   See-ing Je-sus suf-fer loss,
     the heavy cross,   I suffer loss,

All in vain,   All in vain ;   Leaving at the cross my sin,
    All in vain,   All in vain ;   the cross my sin,
Sore dismayed,   Sore dismayed ;   Tak-ing up my cross for God,
    Sore dismayed,   Sore dismayed ;   my cross for God,

Sing-ing as I en-ter in,   Sweet re-frain,   Sweet re-frain.
    I en-ter in,   Sweet refrain,   Sweet refrain.
Sing-ing with my lightened load,   Fears al-layed,   Fears al-layed.
    my lightened load,   Fears al-layed,   Fears allayed.

CHORUS.

Songs of the cross, of the cross, I love to hear, All of their strains are sweet and

clear ;   I'm joy-ous and gladsome, my heart is light and free, Songs of the

Ritard.

cross, of the cross, come sing to me.

3.
Coming to ‖: the river's brink, :‖
Fearful 'mid ‖: the waves I sink, :‖
    Save Thou me,
    Save Thou me ;
Clinging to ‖: the cross I rise, :‖
Shouting to ‖: the upper skies, :‖
    Safe with Thee,
    Safe with Thee.

Words by Rev. W. Hunter.   Music by Asa Hull.

1. There is a spot to me more dear Than na-tive vale or mountain:
2. Hard was my toil to reach the shore, Long toss'd up-on the o-cean;

A spot for which af-fec-tion's tear Springs grateful from its fountain;
A-bove me was the thun-der's roar, Be-neath, the waves' commo-tion;

'Tis not where kin-dred souls a-bound—Tho' that on earth is heav-en—
Dark-ly the pall of night was thrown A-round me, faint with ter-ror;

But where I first my Sav-iour found, And felt my sins for-giv-en.
In that dark hour, how did my groan As-cend from years of er-ror.

3.

Sinking and panting as for breath,
  I knew not help was near me,
And cried, O save me, Lord, from death,
  Immortal Jesus, hear me!
Then quick as tho't I felt Him mine,—
  My Saviour stood before me;
I saw His brightness round me shine,
  And shouted, Glory! Glory!

4.

O sacred hour! O hallowed spot!
  Where love divine first found me;
Wherever falls my distant lot,
  My heart shall linger round thee;
And when from earth at last I soar;
  Up to my home in heaven,
Down will I cast mine eyes once more,
  Where I was first forgiven.

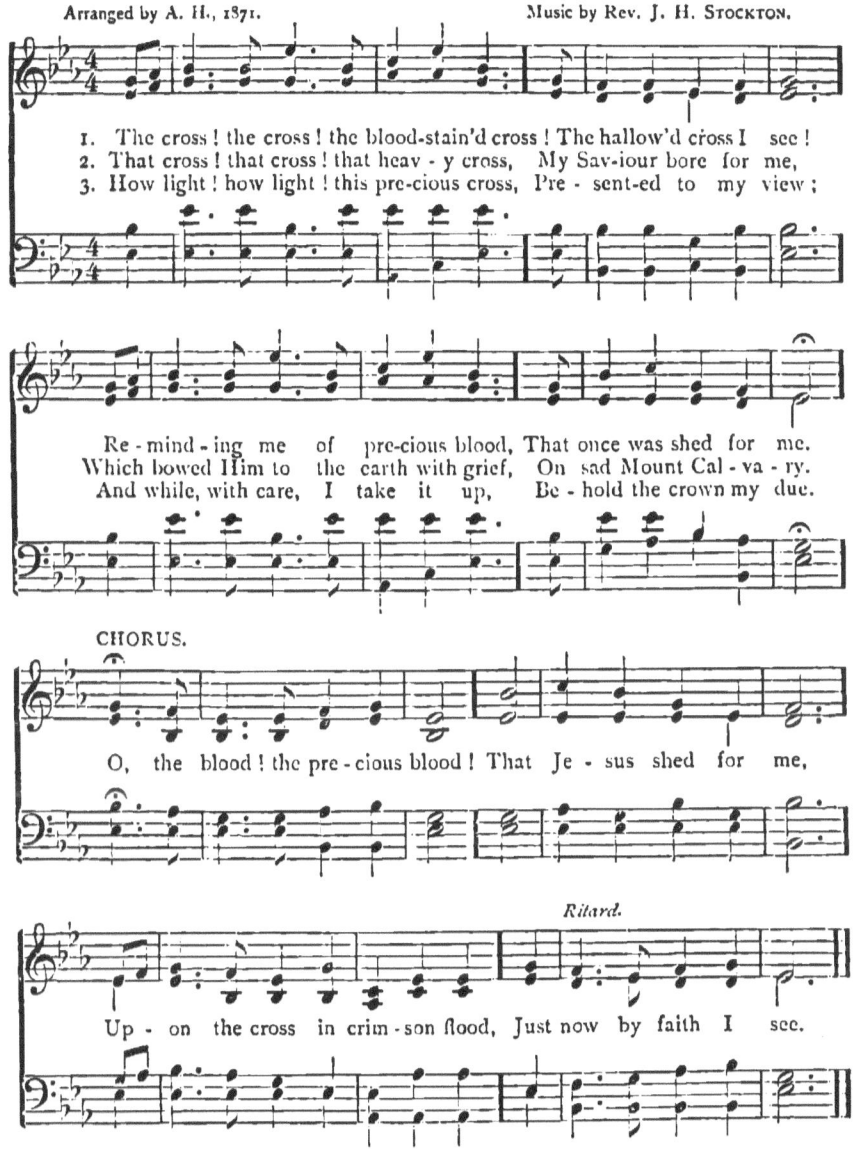

Arranged by A. H., 1871.　　　Music by Rev. J. H. STOCKTON.

1. The cross! the cross! the blood-stain'd cross! The hallow'd cross I see!
2. That cross! that cross! that heav-y cross, My Sav-iour bore for me,
3. How light! how light! this pre-cious cross, Pre-sent-ed to my view;

Re-mind-ing me of pre-cious blood, That once was shed for me.
Which bowed Him to the earth with grief, On sad Mount Cal-va-ry.
And while, with care, I take it up, Be-hold the crown my due.

CHORUS.

O, the blood! the pre-cious blood! That Je-sus shed for me,

Ritard.

Up-on the cross in crim-son flood, Just now by faith I see.

4 The cross! the crown! the glorious
　crown!
　The crown of victory!
　The crown of life! it shall be mine,
　When I shall Jesus see.
　　Cho.—O, the blood, etc.

5 My tears, unbidden, seem to flow
　For love, unbounded love,
　Which guides me through this world
　　of woe,
　And points to joys above.
　　Cho.—O, the blood, etc.

WORK WHILE THE DAY LASTS.

Cheerfully.

Music by Asa Hull.

1. { There are lone-ly hearts to cher - ish, While the days are go - ing by;
   { There are wea-ry souls to per - ish, While the days are go - ing by;

{ If a smile we can re - new,
{ As our jour-ney we pur - sue,

O, the good we all may do,

CHORUS.

While the days are go - ing by. Go - ing, go - ing by, While the

days are going by; Do all the good you can, While the days are going by.

2 There's no time for idle scorning,
  While the days are going by;
Let your face be like the morning,
  While the days are going by;
O, the world is full of sighs,
Full of sad and weeping eyes—
Help your fallen brothers rise,
  While the days are going by.

3 All the loving links that bind us,
  While the days are going by;
One by one we leave behind us,
  While the days are going by;
But the seed of good we sow,
Both in shade and shine will grow,
And will keep our hearts aglow,
  While the days are going by.

Copyright, 1873, by Asa Hull.

From "Palmer's Sab. Sch. Songs." By per.   Words and Music by H. R. PALMER.

1. Yield not to temp-ta - tion, For yielding is sin, Each vic-t'ry will
2. Shun e - vil com-pan - ions, Bad language dis - dain, God's name hold in
3. To him that o'ercom - eth God giv - eth a crown ; Thro' faith we shall

help you Some oth - er to win ; Fight man - ful - ly on - ward,
rev'rence, Nor take it in vain ; Be thought-ful and ear - nest,
con - quer, Though oft - en cast down ; He who is our Sav - iour,

Dark passions sub - due, Look ev - er to Je - sus, He'll car-ry you through.
Kind-heart-ed and true, Look ev - er to Je - sus, He'll car-ry you through.
Our strength will renew, Look ev - er to Je - sus, He'll car-ry you through.

CHORUS.

Ask the Sav-iour to help you, Com-fort, strengthen, and keep you ;

He is will - ing to aid you, He will car - ry you through.

THANKS BE TO GOD.

Words by H. S. Perkins.

Music by Asa Hull.

1. Thanks be to God for the vic - t'ry o - ver sin ; Thanks for His Word and the
2. Thanks for the gift of His loved, His on-ly Son ; Thanks for the work which on
3. Thanks for redemption and purchase by His blood ; Thanks for the love He has

teachings therein ; Thanks for His Son who was giv-en to proclaim Ti - dings of
earth He be - gun ; Thanks for the peace which it brings unto the soul, Working for
taught in His Word ; Thanks for His Spirit, for ev-er-more to reign, Peace on the

CHORUS.

good, and the earth to reclaim. Sing, Sing,
Je - sus, His love to un-fold.
earth, and good will un-to men. Sing a glad ho-san-na, Sing a glad ho-san-na,

Sing for the vic - t'ry o - ver sin ; Sing a glad ho-san-na,
Sing a glad ho-san-na, Sing ho-san-na,

Sing a glad ho-san-na ! Ho-san - na ! ho-san-na ! ho-san - na !
Sing ho-san-na !

Words by Mrs. E. C. Ellsworth.   Music by J. H. Tenney.

1. There were ten that besought Him, the Master di-vine, There were ten that were
2. There were ten who were cleansed, all but one went their way, Were content with the
3. There was grace for the ten, what a marvel that nine Should have turned from the

healed, but where are the nine? On-ly one saw the gift, on-ly one heard the call,
good that lasts but a day; And would you like the nine ever sat-is-fied be,
gift—the treasure di-vine! What a wonder so ma-ny are do-ing the same,

CHORUS.

On-ly one grasped the treasure, tho' offered to all.   O where are the nine to
With a bless-ing so transient, while mercy is free?
By neg-lect-ing sal-va-tion—for them Jesus came.

bow at His feet?   O where are the nine, with grat-i-tude meet? O where are the

ma-ny who own Him divine, But give Him no glo-ry? O where are the nine?

SCATTER SEEDS OF KINDNESS.

Words by Mrs. ALBERT SMITH.

Music by S. J. VAIL.

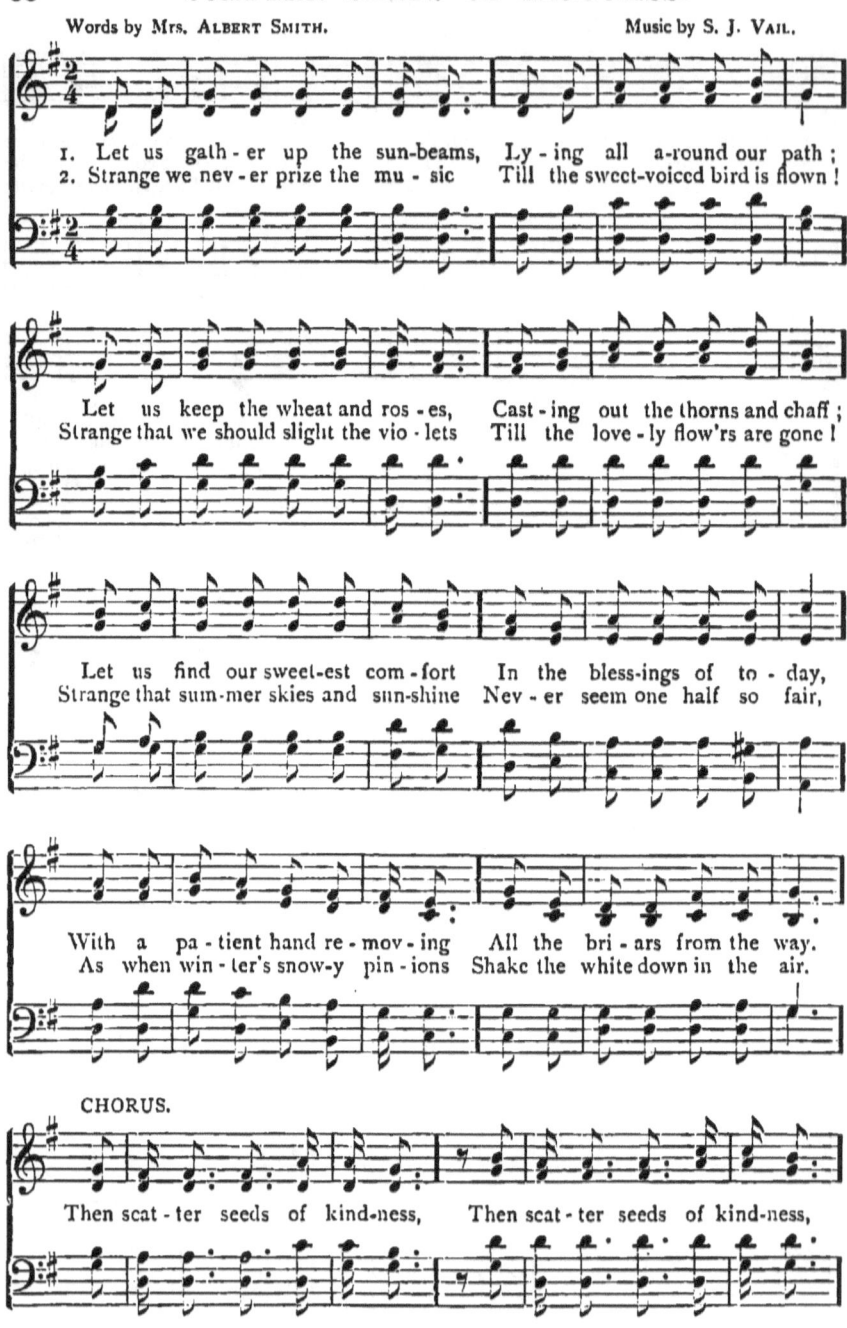

1. Let us gath-er up the sun-beams, Ly-ing all a-round our path ;
2. Strange we nev-er prize the mu-sic Till the sweet-voiced bird is flown !

Let us keep the wheat and ros-es, Cast-ing out the thorns and chaff ;
Strange that we should slight the vio-lets Till the love-ly flow'rs are gone !

Let us find our sweet-est com-fort In the bless-ings of to-day,
Strange that sum-mer skies and sun-shine Nev-er seem one half so fair,

With a pa-tient hand re-mov-ing All the bri-ars from the way.
As when win-ter's snow-y pin-ions Shake the white down in the air.

CHORUS.

Then scat-ter seeds of kind-ness, Then scat-ter seeds of kind-ness,

Then scat-ter seeds of kind-ness For our reap-ing by and by.

3 If we knew the baby fingers,
　Pressed against the window pane,
Would be cold and stiff to-morrow,—
　Never trouble us again,—
Would the bright eyes of our darling
　Catch the frown upon our brow?—
Would the prints of rosy fingers
　Vex us then as they do now?—*Cho.*

4 Ah! those little ice-cold fingers,
　How they point the memories back
To the hasty words and actions
　Strewn around our backward track!
How these little hands remind us,
　As in snowy grace they lie,
Not to scatter thorns, but roses,
　For our reaping by and by.—*Cho.*

DEAR LORD, REMEMBER ME.

From "Palm Leaves."　　　　　　　Music and Cho. by Asa Hull.

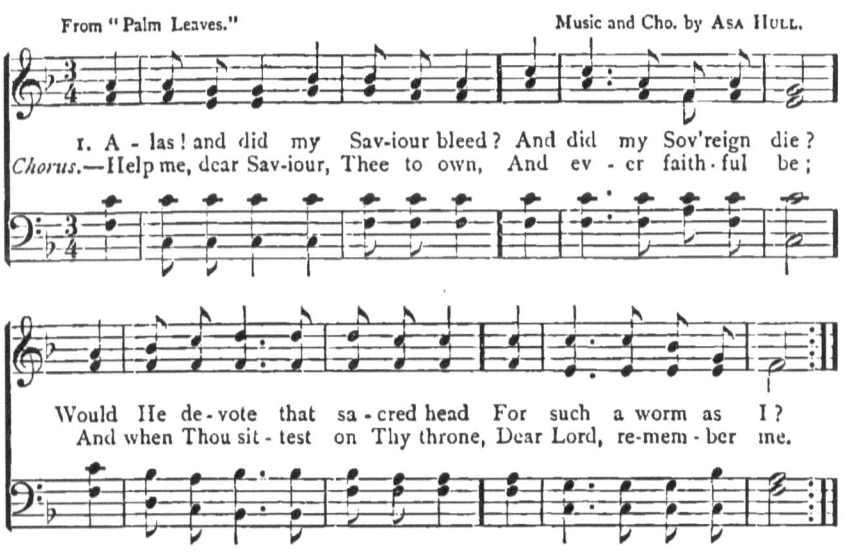

1. A-las! and did my Sav-iour bleed? And did my Sov'reign die?
Chorus.—Help me, dear Sav-iour, Thee to own, And ev-er faith-ful be;

Would He de-vote that sa-cred head For such a worm as I?
And when Thou sit-test on Thy throne, Dear Lord, re-mem-ber me.

2 Was it for crimes that I have done
　He groaned upon a tree?
Amazing pity! grace unknown!
　And love beyond degree.—*Cho.*

3 Well might the sun in darkness hide,
　And shut his glory in,
When Christ, the mighty Maker, died
　For man, the creature's, sin.—*Cho.*

4 Thus might I hide my blushing face
　While His dear cross appears;
Dissolve my heart in thankfulness,
　And melt mine eyes to tears.—*Cho.*

5 But drops of grief can ne'er repay
　The debt of love I owe;
Here, Lord, I give myself away,—
　'Tis all that I can do.—*Cho.*

ALL FOR JESUS!

Words by MARY D. JAMES.   For Mixed Voices.   Music by ASA HULL.

1. All for Je - sus! all for Je - sus! All my being's ransom'd pow'rs;
   All my thoughts and words and doings, All my days and all my hours.

All for Je - sus! all for Je - sus! All my days and all my hours.

2 Let my hands perform His bidding ;
   Let my feet run in His ways ;
   Let my eyes see Jesus only ;
   Let my lips speak forth His praise.
   All for Jesus! all for Jesus!
   Let my lips speak forth His praise.

3 Worldings prize their gems of beauty,
   Cling to gilded toys of dust,
   Boast of wealth, and fame, and pleasure;
   Only Jesus will I trust.
   Only Jesus! only Jesus!
   Only Jesus will I trust.

4 Since my eyes were fixed on Jesus,
   I've lost sight of all beside,—
   So enchained my spirit's vision,
   Looking at the crucified.
   All for Jesus ! all for Jesus !
   All for Jesus, crucified !

5 O, what wonder ! how amazing !
   Jesus, glorious King of kings,
   Deigns to call me His beloved,
   Lets me rest beneath His wings.
   All for Jesus ! all for Jesus !
   Resting now beneath His wings.

ALL FOR JESUS!

1ST AND 2D TENOR.   For Male Voices.   Music by ASA HULL.

Words by S. F. BENNETT.   Music by J. P. WEBSTER.

1. There's a land that is fair - er than day, And by faith we can see it a - far;
2. We shall sing on that beau-ti-ful shore The me-lo - di-ous songs of the blest,
3. To our boun-ti- ful Fa - ther a - bove, We will of - fer the trib-ute of praise,

For the Father waits o - ver the way, To prepare us a dwelling-place there.
And our spir-its shall sorrow no more, Not a sigh for the blessing of rest.
For the glo - ri-ous gift of His love, And the blessings that hallow our days.

CHORUS.

In the sweet   by and by,   We shall meet on that beautiful shore ;
In the sweet by and by, by and by,   by and by,

In the sweet   by and by,   We shall meet on that beauti-ful shore.
In the sweet by and by, by and by,

4.
We shall rest on that beautiful shore,
    In the joys of the saved we shall share ;
All our pilgrimage toil will be o'er,
    And the conqueror's crown we shall
        wear.
    Chorus.—In the sweet, etc.

5.
We shall meet, we shall sing, we shall
        reign,
    In the land where the saved never die ;
We shall rest free from sorrow and pain,
    Safe at home in the sweet by and by.—
    Chorus.—In the sweet, etc.

THE REAPERS.

Words by Asa Hull.
Moderato.

Music by Asa Hull.
Chorus suggested by another melody.

1. Be-hold the changing autumn leaves, Be-hold the fields of rip'ning grain,
2. Be-hold the har-vest of the Lord! Behold the broad and whitening fields!
3. Why i-dly stand? there's work for all; The Master calls, why lon-ger wait?

Go gath-er in the gold-en sheaves From val-ley, hill, and dis-tant plain.
Send out the call, send forth the word, Till hun-dred-fold the har-vest yields.
Go, gath-er in both great and small, Make haste, or you will be too late.

CHORUS.—*A little faster.*

Then, reap-ers, haste,............ the skies are clear,............
Then, reap-ers, haste, *the skies are clear,*

The fields re-sound............ the glad re-frain............
The fields re-sound *the glad re-frain,*

The har-vest-ers,............ from far and near,............
The har-vest-ers, *from far and near,*

Rit.

Are gath-'ring in.............. the gold - en grain............

Are gath-'ring in the gold - en grain, the gold - en grain.

CORONATION. C. M.

Words by Perronet.

Music by O. Holden.

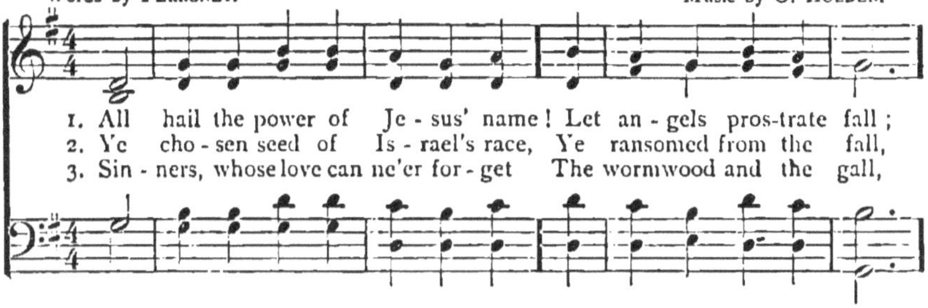

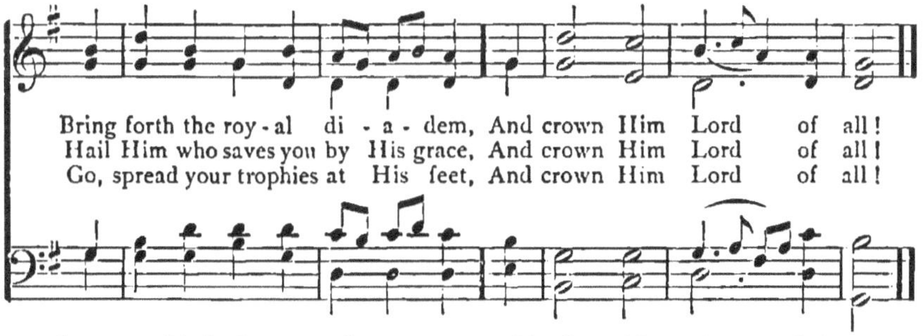

1. All hail the power of Je - sus' name! Let an - gels pros-trate fall;
2. Ye cho - sen seed of Is - rael's race, Ye ransomed from the fall,
3. Sin - ners, whose love can ne'er for - get The wormwood and the gall,

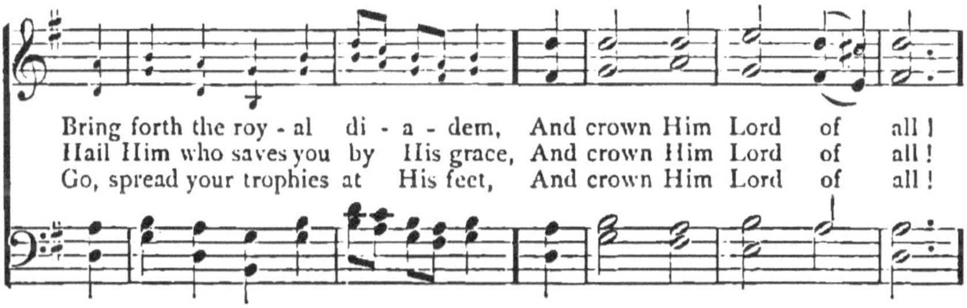

Bring forth the roy - al di - a - dem, And crown Him Lord of all !
Hail Him who saves you by His grace, And crown Him Lord of all !
Go, spread your trophies at His feet, And crown Him Lord of all !

Bring forth the roy - al di - a - dem, And crown Him Lord of all !
Hail Him who saves you by His grace, And crown Him Lord of all !
Go, spread your trophies at His feet, And crown Him Lord of all !

4 Let every kindred, every tribe,
On this terrestrial ball,
To Him all majesty ascribe,
And crown Him Lord of all !

5 Oh, that with yonder sacred throng,
We at His feet may fall !
We'll join the everlasting song,
And crown Him Lord of all !

TALKING WITH JESUS.

Adagio, Eepressivo.

Music by Asa Hull.

1. A lit - tle talk with Je - sus, How it smoothes the rug-ged road ;
2. I know the way is drear - y To that bright and hap - py clime ;

How it seems to help me on - ward, When I faint be-neath my load.
But a lit - tle talk with Je - sus Will re - fresh me an - y time.

When my heart is crushed with sor - row, And my eyes with tears are dim,
And as yet the more I know Him, And His mer - cy I ex - plore,

There is naught can yield me com - fort Like a lit - tle talk with Him.
On - ly prompts my heart to long - ing For a lit - tle talk the more.

CHORUS.

O I love to talk with Je - sus, For earth - ly joys grow dim ;

And there's naught can yield me comfort, Like a lit-tle talk with Him.

3 I'll tell Him I am weary,
  And I fain would be at rest ;
  That I'm daily, hourly longing
  For a home upon His breast.
  Once He gave His life a ransom,
  And would have me all His own,
  Can He now forget His promise,
  And reject His purchased one ?

4 I'll wait a little longer,—
  Till His own appointed time ;
  And will glory in the knowledge
  Of a prospect so sublime.
  Then, when in my Father's dwelling,
  Where the many "mansions" are,
  I will sweetly talk with Jesus,
  And forever dwell up there.

Copyright, 1876, *by* ASA HULL.

ROCK OF AGES.

Words by TOPLADY. Arr.　　　　　　Music by Dr. T. HASTINGS. Arr.

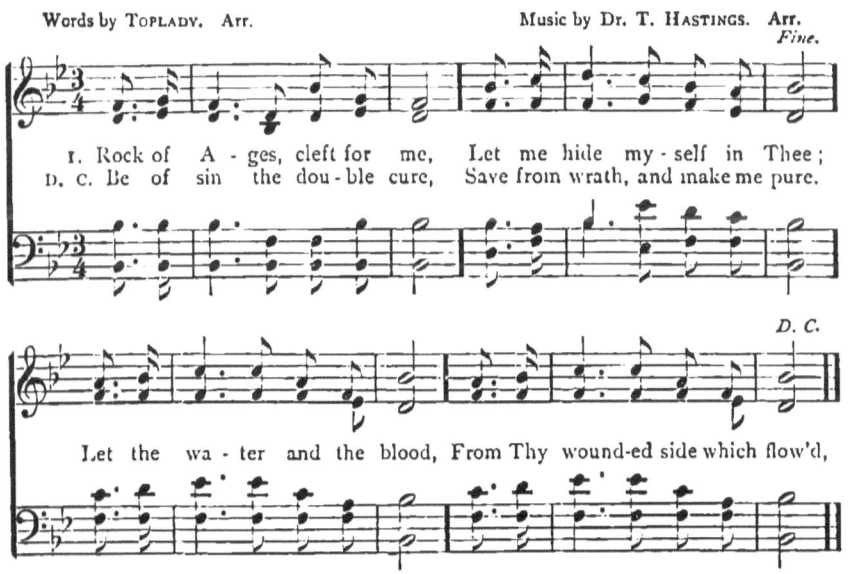

1. Rock of A - ges, cleft for me, Let me hide my-self in Thee ;
D. C. Be of sin the dou-ble cure, Save from wrath, and make me pure.

Let the wa-ter and the blood, From Thy wound-ed side which flow'd,

2 Could my tears for ever flow,
  Could my zeal no longer know,
  These for sin could not atone :
  Thou must save, and Thou alone :
  In my hand no price I bring ;
  Simply to Thy cross I cling.

3 While I draw this fleeting breath,
  When my eyes shall close in death,
  When I rise to worlds unknown,
  And behold Thee on Thy throne,—
  Rock of Ages, cleft for me,
  Let me hide myself in Thee.

I REST IN THY LOVE.

Words by Rev. R. W. Todd.   Music by Harry Sanders.

1. While way-worn and wea-ry, I jour-ney a-long, Dear Sav-iour, Thy
2. While burden'd with sor-row, and lad-en'd with woe; Dear Sav-iour, to

love is the theme of my song; Thy smile is my bea-con, as
Thee, 'neath Thy cross will I go; I think of Thy sor-row, and

on-ward I move; Thy cross is my shel-ter, I rest in Thy love.
an-guish for me, And yield at Thy bid-ding, my sor-rows to Thee.

CHORUS.

I rest in Thy love,.... yes, rest in Thy love,.... Tho' way-worn and
Rest in Thy love,   Rest in Thy love,

rit. pp

wea-ry, I rest in Thy love, Rest in Thy love, yes, rest in Thy love.
Rest in Thy love,   in Thy love.

Copyright, 1879, by Asa Hull.

Andantino.

Music by Dr. L. Mason.

1. Near-er, my God, to Thee, Nearer to Thee, E'en tho' it be a cross
2. Though like a wan-derer, Day-light all gone, Darkness be o - ver me,
3. There let the way appear Steps up to heav'n : All that Thou sendest me

That rais - eth me ; Still all my song shall be, Near - er, my
My rest a stone ; Yet in my dreams I'd be, Near - er, etc.
In mer - cy giv'n : An - gels to beck - on me Near - er, etc.

God, to Thee, Near - er, my God, to Thee, Near - er to Thee.

4 Then, with my waking thoughts,
　Bright with Thy praise,
Out of my stony griefs,
　Bethel I'll raise ;
So by my woes to be
‖: Nearer, my God, to Thee,:‖
　Nearer to Thee.

5 Or, if on joyful wing,
　Cleaving the sky,
Sun, moon and stars forgot,
　Upward I fly,—
Still all my song shall be,
‖: Nearer my God, to Thee,:‖
　Nearer to Thee.

CONCLUSION OF **I REST IN THY LOVE,** OPPOSITE PAGE.

3 While struggling for Thee in the heat of the strife,
　Dear Saviour, Thy truth is the shield of my life ;
　My foes shall be vanquished—shall die 'neath my feet ;
　I'll rest from the conflict with vict'ry complete.—*Chorus*

4 And when,—all the pangs of mortality o'er,—
　I'll join with the blood-washed who sing on the shore ;
　I'll dwell with the pure in Thy temple above ;
　Forever and ever I'll rest in Thy love.—*Chorus.*

Words by Miss P. J. Owens.   From " Praise Songs."   Music by Asa Hull.

1. When sail - ing o'er time's rest - less sea,   Be - neath a cloud-ed sky ;
2. Loud raves the voice of an - gry gales,   But while the breakers foam,
3. Then let the frown-ing clouds grow dark,   The tem - pest wild - ly rave ;

How sweet the whis-per comes to me,   A Sav - iour ev - er nigh.
A   soft wind fans the spreading sails, The pleasant breeze from home.
A   strong hand guides the lad - en bark A - cross the storm-y wave.

Breezes from the heav'nly land, They sweep across the sea ; They waft the mu-sic
Breezes from the heav'nly land, They sweep the billows o'er, The voi - ces of a
Breezes from the heav'nly land, They murmur o'er the wave, The wel-come of an

CHORUS. *Animato.*

on the strand, The song of hope to me.   O, wait-ing souls, re-joice, We're
lov - ing band Are waft - ed from the shore.
outstretched hand, A heart that bled to save.

near the ho-ly strand, List! 'tis the Saviour's voice, The welcome breeze from land.

Copyright, 1871, *by* Asa Hull.

Music by JOHN M. EVANS.

1. "Land a - head!" its fruits are wav-ing O'er the hills of fade-less green;
2. On-ward, bark, the cape I'm rounding; See the bless - ed wave their hands;

And the liv - ing wa - ters lav - ing Shores where heav'nly forms are seen.
Hear the harps of God re-sound-ing From the bright, im - mor - tal bands.

CHORUS.

Rocks and storms I'll fear no more, When on that e - ter - nal shore;

Drop the an - chor! furl the sail! I am safe with-in the vail!

3 There, let go the anchor, riding
On this calm and silv'ry bay;
Seaward fast the tide is gliding;
Shores in sunlight stretch away.
  Cho.—Rocks and storms, etc.

4 Now we're safe from all temptation;
All the storms of life are past;
Praise the Rock of our salvation!
We are safe at home at last!
  Cho.—Rocks and storms, etc.

Solo or Quartette.
Arranged. Music by Franz Abt.

1. Guide me, O Thou great Je - ho - vah, Pil - grim through this bar - ren land;
2. O - pen now the crys - tal foun - tain, Whence the heal - ing wa - ters flow;

I am weak, but Thou art might - y, Hold me with Thy power-ful hand:
Let the fi - ery, cloud - y pil - lar Lead me all my jour - ney thro';

Bread of heav - en, Bread of heav-en, Feed me till I want no more;
Strong De - liv - 'rer, Strong De-liv - 'rer, Be Thou still my strength and shield;

Full Chorus.

Bread of heav - en, Bread of heaven, Feed me till I want no more,
Strong De - liv - 'rer, Strong De - liv - 'rer, Be Thou still my strength and shield,

Feed me till I want no more.
Be Thou still my strength and shield.

3.

When I tread the verge of Jordan
Bid my anxious fears subside,
Bear me through the swelling current,
Land me safe on Canaan's side :
Songs of praises, Songs of praises,
I will ever give to Thee ;
Songs of praises, Songs of praises,
I will ever give to Thee.
I will ever give to Thee.

Words by Mrs. E. C. ELLSWORTH. Music by J. H. TENNEY.

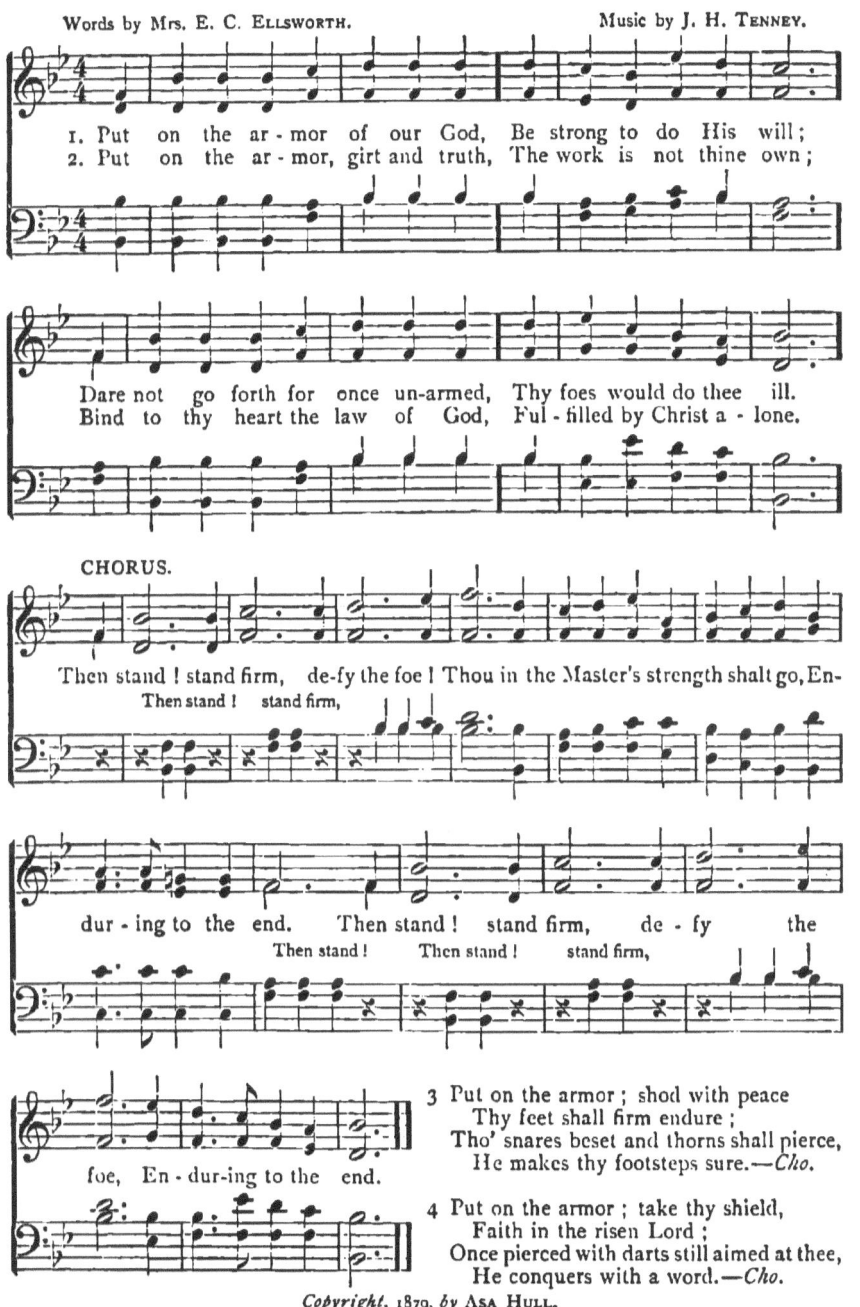

1. Put on the ar - mor of our God, Be strong to do His will;
2. Put on the ar - mor, girt and truth, The work is not thine own;

Dare not go forth for once un-armed, Thy foes would do thee ill.
Bind to thy heart the law of God, Ful - filled by Christ a - lone.

CHORUS.

Then stand ! stand firm, de-fy the foe ! Thou in the Master's strength shalt go, En-
Then stand ! stand firm,

dur - ing to the end. Then stand ! stand firm, de - fy the
Then stand ! Then stand ! stand firm,

foe, En - dur-ing to the end.

3 Put on the armor ; shod with peace
  Thy feet shall firm endure ;
  Tho' snares beset and thorns shall pierce,
  He makes thy footsteps sure.—*Cho.*

4 Put on the armor ; take thy shield,
  Faith in the risen Lord ;
  Once pierced with darts still aimed at thee,
  He conquers with a word.—*Cho.*

NO BOOK IS LIKE THE BIBLE.

Words by FANNY J. CROSBY.

Music by ASA HULL.

1. No book is like the Bi - ble, For childhood, youth and age ; Our duty, plain and
2. It tells of man's cre-a-tion, His sad, pri-me-val fall ; It tells of man's re-
3. O, let us love the Bi - ble, And praise it more and more ; Our life is like a

sim - ple, We find on ev -'ry page ; It came by in - spi - ra - tion ; A
demp-tion, Thro' Christ, who died for all ; In sa - cred words of wis - dom It
shad - ow, Our days will soon be o'er ; But if we close-ly fol - low The

light to guide our way, A voice from Him who gave it, Reproving when we stray.
bids us watch and pray, And early come to Jesus, The Life, the Truth, the Way.
counsel God has giv-en, We then may hope with angels To sing His praise in heaven.

CHORUS.

No book is like the Bi - ble, The bless - ed book we love,

The pil-grim's chart of glo - ry, It leads to God a - bove.

WILL IT, O LORD, BE MINE?

Words by Mrs. E. C. ELLSWORTH.　　　　　　Music by J. H. TENNEY.

Moderato.

1. There's joy for the soul when the Master has come, Will it be mine? Will it be mine?
2. There's rest for the soul when its race has been run, Will it be mine? Will it be mine?

There's joy in re-un-ion, when all are at home, Will it, O Lord, be mine?
There's rest for the soul when with sin it has done, Will it, O Lord, be mine?

Joy in the welcome to yonder bright shore, Joy in the meetings where partings are o'er;
Rest for the weary, with burdens oppressed, Rest for the toiler, with patience possessed,

Joy in the greet-ing of friends gone before, Will it, O Lord, be mine?
Rest in the Lord, O the sweetest and best; Will it, O Lord, etc.

Slower.

Will it be mine? Will it be mine? Will it, O Lord, be mine?

BURNING THE CHAFF.

Words by Rev. H. R. Trickett.　　　　　　　　　Music by J. H. Rosecrans.

1. Min-gled to-geth-er the wheat and the chaff, Waiting their doom in the
2. Gath-'ring the wheat for the gar-ner of God, Rob-ing the vic-tors in
3. On-ly the wick-ed shall be as the chaff; Now is the time when dear

day of His ire; Soon will the Mighty One win-now His threshing-floor,
gar-ments of light; Nev-er to sin a-gain, nev-er to sor-row more,
sin-ners may turn; Soon will they pass be-yond mer-cy's redeeming power,

CHORUS.

Wheat for His gar-ner, the chaff for the fire. Burn-ing the chaff in the
Stand-ing for-ev-er approved in His sight.
And found among the chaff, like chaff must they burn.

day of His wrath, Purging His floor with His fan in His hand; Burning the

chaff with un-quench-a-ble fire, Who in that day will be a-ble to stand?

Words and Music by W. J. KIRKPATRICK.

1. Je - sus, Sav - iour, great Ex-am - ple, Pat - tern of all pu - ri - ty,
2. Lest I wan - der from Thy path-way, Or my feet move wea - ri - ly,
3. When temp-ta-tions fierce-ly low - er, And my shrinking soul would flee,

I would fol - low in thy foot - steps, Dai - ly grow-ing more like Thee.
Sav - iour, take my hand and lead me, Keep me steadfast : more like Thee.
Change each weakness in - to pow - er, Keep me spot - less : more like Thee.

CHORUS.

More like Thee, more like Thee ; Sav-iour, this my constant prayer shall be—
More like Thee, more like Thee:

Day by day, where'er I stray, Make me more and more like Thee.

4 When around me all is darkness,
   And Thy beauties none may see,
May Thy beams, O glorious Brightness,
   In effulgence shine through me.
    Cho.—More like Thee, etc.

5 When death's cold, repulsive finger
   Leaves its impress on my brow,
May Thy life, within me swelling,
   Keep me singing then as now.
    Cho.—More like Thee, etc.

FLEE TO YOUR MOUNTAIN.

Words by Mrs. S. B. Dana.

Music by Asa Hull.

1. Flee as a bird to your mountain, Thou who art wea-ry of sin;
2. He will pro-tect thee for ev - er, Wipe ev-'ry sad, fall-ing tear;

Go to the clear, flow-ing foun - tain, Where you may wash and be clean;
He will for-sake thee, O, nev - er, Cher-ish'd so ten - der-ly there:

Fly, for th'a-veng-er is near thee; Call, and the Saviour will hear thee;
Loose not the hours that are fly - ing; Spend not the moments in sigh - ing;

Slow. Ral - len - tan - do.

He on His bo - som will bear thee; O thou who art wea-ry of sin,
Cease from your sor-row and cry - ing; The Sav-iour will wipe ev-'ry tear,

A tempo.

O thou who art wea - ry of sin.
The Saviour will wipe ev'ry tear,

3.
Come, then, to Jesus, thy Saviour :
He will redeem thee from sin,
Bless with a sense of His favor,
Make thee all glorious within ;
Call, for the Saviour is near thee,
Waiting in mercy to hear thee,
And by His presence to cheer thee,
|: O thou who art weary of sin. :|

Copyright, 1865, by Asa Hull.

Words by H. L. HASTINGS.   Music by E. S. RICE. From the "Little Sower."

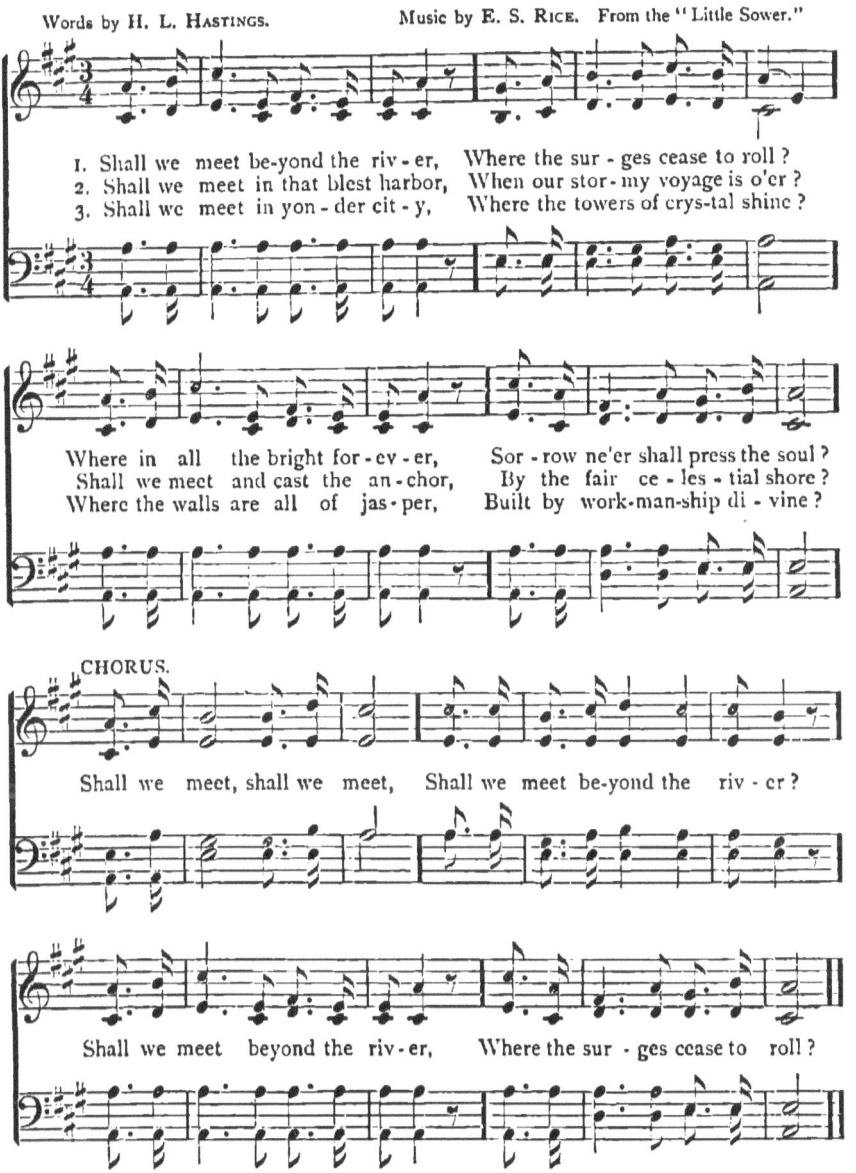

1. Shall we meet be-yond the riv-er, Where the sur-ges cease to roll?
2. Shall we meet in that blest harbor, When our stor-my voyage is o'er?
3. Shall we meet in yon-der cit-y, Where the towers of crys-tal shine?

Where in all the bright for-ev-er, Sor-row ne'er shall press the soul?
Shall we meet and cast the an-chor, By the fair ce-les-tial shore?
Where the walls are all of jas-per, Built by work-man-ship di-vine?

CHORUS.

Shall we meet, shall we meet, Shall we meet be-yond the riv-er?

Shall we meet beyond the riv-er, Where the sur-ges cease to roll?

4 Shall we meet with many a loved one,
That was torn from our embrace?
Shall we listen to their voices,
And behold them face to face?
Chorus.—Shall we meet, etc.

5 Shall we meet with Christ our Saviour,
When He comes to claim His own?
Shall we know His blessed favor,
And sit down upon His throne?
Chorus.—We shall meet, etc.

THE FOUNTAIN OF MERCY.

Words by H. Q. Wilson.   Music by Asa Hull.

1. 'Twas Je - sus, my Saviour, who died on a tree, To o - pen a
Cho.— For the Li - on of Ju - dah shall break ev - 'ry chain, And give us the
[has bro - ken,]   [gives]

foun - tain for sin - ners like me ; His blood is that foun - tain, which
vic - t'ry a - gain and a - gain ; For the Li - on of Ju - dah shall
[has

Rit. un poco.

par - don be - stows, And cleanses the foul - est wher - ev - er it flows,
break ev' - ry chain, And give us the vic - t'ry a - gain and a - gain.
broken]   [gives]

2 And when I was willing with all things to part,
  He gave me my bounty,—His love in my heart ;
  So now I am joined with the conquering band
  Who are marching to glory at Jesus' command.
  Chorus.—For the Lion of Judah, etc.

3 Though round me the storms of adversity roll,
  And the waves of destruction encompass my soul,
  In vain this frail vessel the tempest shall toss ;
  My hopes rest secure on the blood of the cross.
  Chorus.—For the Lion of Judah, etc.

4 And when the last trumpet of judgment shall sound,
  And wake all the nations that sleep in the ground,
  Then, when heaven and earth shall be melting away,
  I'll sing of the blood of the cross in that day.
  Chorus.—For the Lion of Judah, etc.

5 And when with the ransomed by Jesus, my head,
  From fountain to fountain I then shall be led ;
  I'll fall at His feet and His mercy adore,
  And sing of the blood of the cross evermore.
  Chorus.—For the Lion of Judah, etc.

Music by Dr. L. MASON.

1. Work, for the night is com - ing, Work through the morn - ing hours,
2. Work, for the night is com - ing, Work through the sun - ny noon ;

Work while the dew is spark - ling, Work 'mid spring - ing flow'rs ;
Fill bright-est hours with la - bor,— Rest comes sure and soon :

Work, when the day grows bright - er, Work in the glow - ing sun ;
Give ev' - ry fly - ing min - ute Some - thing to keep in store ;

Work, for the night is com - ing, When man's work is done.
Work, for the night is com - ing, When man work no more.

3 Work, for the night is coming,
    Under the sunset skies ;
  While their bright tints are glowing,
    Work, for the daylight flies ;
  Work, till the last beam fadeth,
    Fadeth to shine no more ;
  Work, while the night is dark'ning,
    When man's work is o'er.

4 Work, for the night is coming,
    Work, while the fields are white ;
  Work, for thy sands are running,
    Work, while hopes are bright ;
  Gather thy sheaves of morning ;
    Rest not thy hand at noon ;
  Labor and strive till ev'ning ;
    Rest when daylight's gone.

THE HARPERS OF GOD.

Words by Rev. H. R. Trickett.　　　　　　　　　Music by J. H. Rosecrans.

1. With crowns on their heads and with harps in their hands, And robed in white raiment the
2. For Thou hast redeemed us from sin by Thy blood, By grace we are made kings and

glo - ri - fied stand ; They are har-pers of God and for - ev - er they sing
priests un - to God ;　O !.... strike ev - 'ry chord, and let heav - en　a - gain

CHORUS.

All wor-thy, all wor-thy our Sav-iour and King.　O sing-ers of heaven ! O
Resound with the praise of the Lamb that was slain.

glo - ri-fied throng ! O spotless and ho - ly ones, harpers of God ! By faith I can

see you　and join　in your song, The song of　redemption, sal - va - tion by blood.

By permission.   Music by Rev. L. HARTSOUGH.

1. I hear Thy welcome voice, That calls me, Lord, to Thee ; For cleansing in Thy
2. Tho' coming weak and vile, Thou dost my strength assure; Thou dost my vileness
3. 'Tis Je - sus calls me on To per-fect faith and love, To perfect hope, and

CHORUS.

prec-ious blood, That flow'd on Cal - va - ry.   I am com - ing, Lord !
ful - ly cleanse, Till spot-less all, and pure.
peace, and trust, For earth and heav'n a - bove.

Com - ing now to Thee ! Wash me, cleanse me, in the blood That flow'd on Calvary.

4 And He the witness gives
  To loyal hearts and free,
That every promise is fulfilled,
  If faith but brings the plea.
  Cho.—I am coming, etc.

5 All hail ! atoning blood !
  All hail ! redeeming grace !
All hail ! the gift of Christ, our Lord,
  Our Strength and Righteousness.
  Cho.—I am coming, etc.

CONCLUSION OF **THE HARPERS OF GOD,** OPPOSITE PAGE.

3 O harpers of God, hallelujah I cry,
  I join in the chorus that rings through the sky ;
  I too am forgiven, I'm saved by the blood,
  I love Him, I own Him my Lord and my God.—*Chorus.*

4 O glorified singers, through Jesus I come,
  To join you, and rest in my heavenly home ;
  I long for the moment, it cannot be long,
  When rising in rapture I join in your song.—*Chorus.*

THE BEAUTIFUL STREAM.

Words by R. Torrey, Jr. *May be used as Soprano Solo.* Music by Asa Hull.

1. O have you not heard of a beautiful stream, That's flowing thro' our Father's land?
2. With murmuring sound doth it wander along, Thro' fields arrayed in liv-ing green;

Its waters gleam bright in the heavenly light, And ripple o'er golden sand.
Where songs of the blest, in their haven of rest, Float soft on the air se - rene.

CHORUS.

That beau - ti - ful stream.... is the "Riv - er of Life,"......
That beau-ti-ful stream is the "Riv-er of Life," That beau-ti-ful stream is the "Riv-er of Life,"

It flows for all na - tions, it flows for all na-tions free;
It flows for all na-tions, it flows for all na-tions,

A balm for each wound in its water is found, O sin-ner, it flows for thee!
for thee!

Words by Watts. Music arr. from Handel.

1. Joy to the world, the Lord is come! Let earth re-ceive her King;

Let ev - 'ry heart pre - pare Him room, And heav'n and nature sing, And

And heav'n and nature

heav'n and na - ture sing, And heav'n, and heav'n and na - ture sing.

sing,......................................

And heav'n and na - ture sing,

2 Joy to the world, the Saviour reigns ;
Let men their songs employ ;
While fields and floods, rocks, hills and
Repeat the sounding joy.   [plains

3 No more let sin and sorrow grow,
Nor thorns infest the ground ;

He comes to make His blessings flow
Far as the curse is found.

4 He rules the world with truth and grace,
And makes the nations prove
The glories of His righteousness
And wonders of His love.

CONCLUSION OF **THE BEAUTIFUL STREAM,** OPPOSITE PAGE.

3 Its fountains are deep, and its waters are pure,
And sweet their taste to weary souls ;
It flows from the throne of Jehovah alone !
O, come where its bright wave rolls.—*Chorus.*

4 O will you not drink of this beautiful stream,
And dwell upon its peaceful shore ?
The Spirit says, come, all ye weary ones home,
And wander in sin no more.—*Chorus.*

THE GLORIOUS BY AND BY.

Moderato.

Music by Asa Hull.

1. It may be far, it may be near,—There is a hope, there is a fear,
2. Yes, by and by will soon be now, And God shall wipe each tear-stained brow;

But in the fu - ture wait-ing, I Shall Je - sus see, yes, by and by.
The Lamb shall feed them from the throne; To liv - ing fountains lead His own.

REFRAIN. Rep. pp ad lib.

By and by, yes, by and by,
By and by, yes, by and by,

By and by, yes, by and
By and by, yes, by and by,

Rall.   A tempo.

by,   yes, by and by;) But in the fu - ture wait-ing, I Shall
By and by, yes, by and by;) The Lamb shall feed them from the throne; To

Je - sus see, yes, by and by.
liv - ing fountains lead His own.

3.
O verdant fields ! O shining shore !
The Lamb of God spreads wide the door ;
O golden City ! surely I
Shall see your glories by and by.
By and by, yes, by and by,
By and by, yes, by and by ;
O golden City ! surely I
Shall see your glories by and by.

Copyright, 1872, by Asa Hull.

PLEYEL'S HYMN. 7s.

Music by PLEYEL.

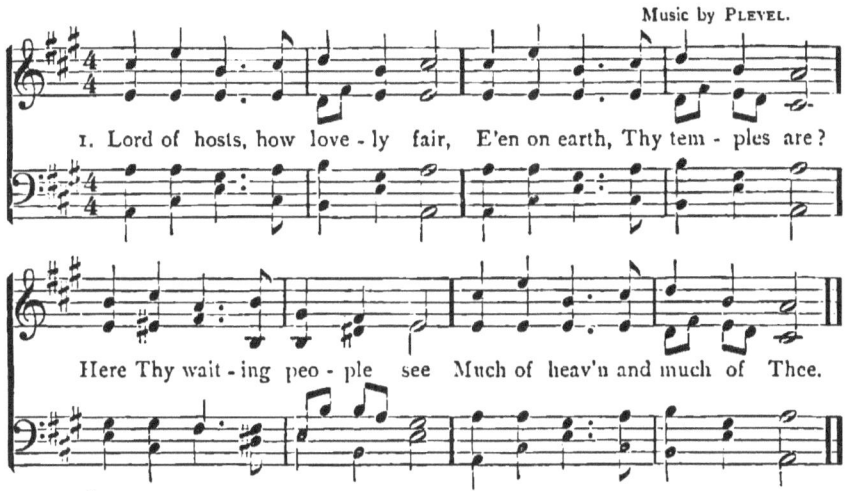

1. Lord of hosts, how love-ly fair, E'en on earth, Thy tem-ples are?

Here Thy wait-ing peo-ple see Much of heav'n and much of Thee.

2 From Thy gracious presence flows
Bliss that softens all our woes;
While Thy Spirit's holy fire
Warms our hearts with pure desire.

3 Here we supplicate Thy throne;
Here Thy pard'ning grace is known;
Here we learn Thy righteous ways,
Taste Thy love, and sing Thy praise.

HURSLEY. L. M.

Words by J. KEBLE.   Arranged from F. J. HAYDN.

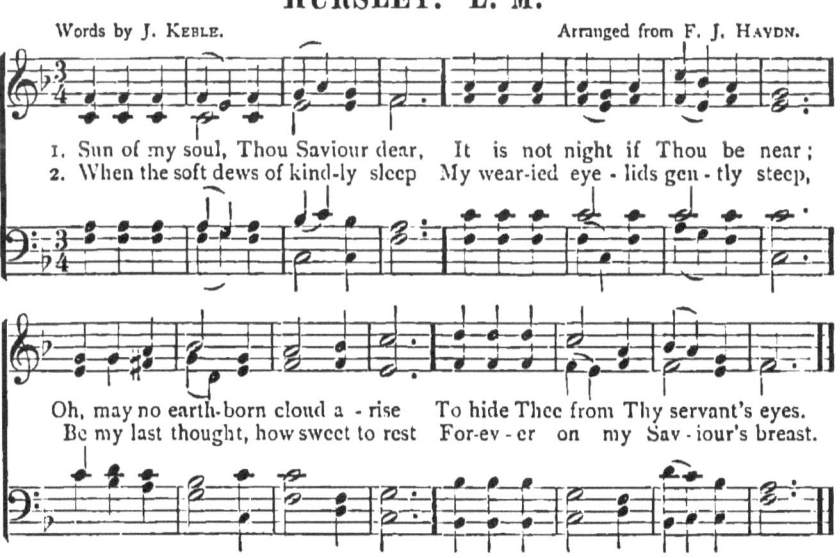

1. Sun of my soul, Thou Saviour dear, It is not night if Thou be near;
2. When the soft dews of kind-ly sleep My wear-ied eye-lids gen-tly steep,

Oh, may no earth-born cloud a-rise To hide Thee from Thy servant's eyes.
Be my last thought, how sweet to rest For-ev-er on my Sav-iour's breast.

3 Abide with me from morn till eve,
For without Thee I cannot live;
Abide with me when death is nigh,
For without Thee I dare not die.

4 If some poor wand'ring child of Thine
Has spurned to-day the voice divine—
Now, Lord, the gracious work begin;
Let Him no more lie down in sin.

JESUS IS CALLING FOR THEE.

Words by GRACE GLENN.　　　　　　　　　　Music by J. H. FILMORE.

1. When, as of old, in her sad - ness, Ma - ry sat weep - ing a - lone,
2. Oh, when thy pleasures are flow - ing, Fad - ing thy hope and thy trust,
3. Down by the shore of death's riv- er, Some time thy foot-steps shall stray,

Soft - ly the voice of her sis - ter Whispered, "The Master has come."
When of the dear - est earth treas-ures Dust shall re - turn un - to dust:
Where waits an an - gel to bear thee O - ver to in - fi - nite day.

So, in the depths of thy sor - row, Gall tho' its foun-tain may be,
Then, tho' the world may in - vite thee, Vain will its of - fer - ing be,
What then tho' dark be his shad - ow, If then his com - ing thou see,

List, for there cometh a whis - per, Je - sus is call - ing for thee.
List, for there cometh a whis - per, Je - sus is call - ing for thee.
Cometh there soft - ly a whis - per, Je - sus is call - ing for thee.

CHORUS. f Rep. pp

Call - - ing, call - - ing, Je - sus is call - ing for thee.
Call - ing for thee, call - ing for thee,

WELCOME TO GLORY.

97

Words by Mrs. P. PALMER. Music by Mrs. J. F. KNAPP.

1. O, when I shall sweep thro' the gate, The scenes of mor-tal-i-ty o'er,
2. When from Calv'ry's mount I a-rise, And pass thro' the por-tals a-bove,
3. Yes! loved ones who knew me below, Who learn'd the new song with me here,

What then for my spir-it a-waits? Will they sing on the glo-ri-fied shore?
Will shout, Welcome home to the skies, Resound thro' the re-gions of love?
In cho-rus will hail me, I know, And welcome me home with good cheer.

CHORUS.

Welcome home! wel-come home! A wel-come in glo-ry for
Wel-come home! Wel-come home!

me; Welcome home! welcome home! A wel-come for me.
Welcome home! Welcome home! Welcome home!

4.
The beautiful gates will unfold,
   The home of the blood-washed I'll see;
The city of saints I'll behold!
   For, O, there's a welcome for me!
   Cho.—Welcome home, etc.

5.
A sinner made whiter than snow,
   I'll join in the mighty acclaim,
And shout through the gates as I go,
   Salvation to God and the Lamb!
   Cho.—Welcome home, etc.

I WILL KNOCK AT THE DOOR.

Words revised.

Music by Rev. D. C. JOHN.

1. The mistakes of my life are ma - ny, And the sins of my heart are more :
2. I'm the low - est of those who love Him ; I'm the weak-est of those who pray ;

I can scarce-ly see for weeping, But still I will knock at the door,
But I come just as He has bid me, And He will not turn me a - way.

CHORUS.

Come in, come in, wea-ry one, come in, Come
Come in, come in, wea - ry one, come in,

in, wea - ry one, The Sav-iour bids you come in.
Come in, wea - ry one,

3 The mistakes of my life are many,
And my spirit is faint with sin;
Yet, 'mid sorrow, I hear Thee whisper,
Come in, weary one, now come in.
Chorus.—Come in, etc.

4 All my sins Jesus will forgive me :
All my stains He will wash away ;
And the feet that so oft have stumbled,
Shall tread thro' the bright gate of day.
Chorus.—Come in, etc.

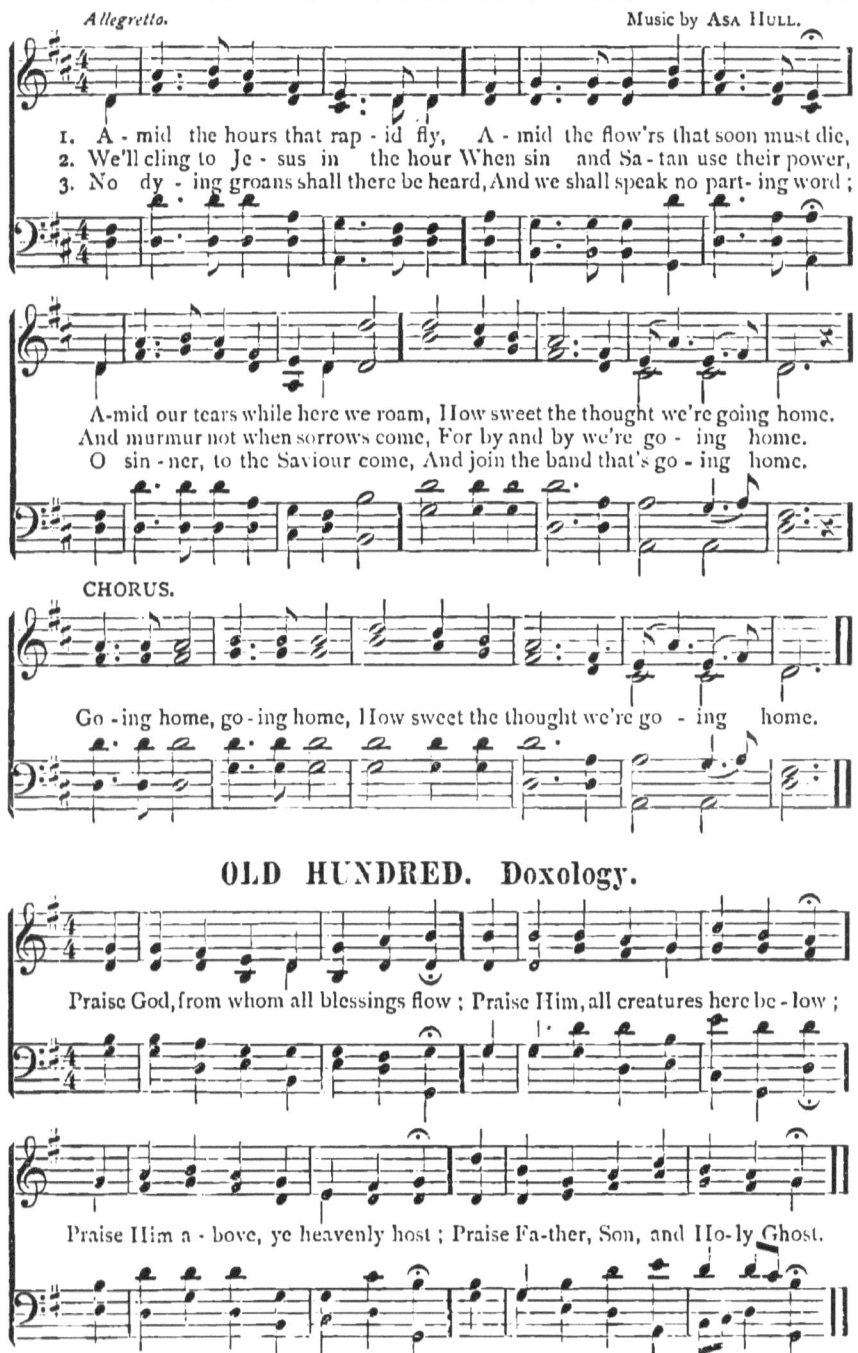

THE GLORIOUS PROSPECT.

Allegretto.   Music by ASA HULL.

1. A - mid the hours that rap - id fly, A - mid the flow'rs that soon must die,
2. We'll cling to Je - sus in the hour When sin and Sa - tan use their power,
3. No dy - ing groans shall there be heard, And we shall speak no part- ing word ;

A-mid our tears while here we roam, How sweet the thought we're going home.
And murmur not when sorrows come, For by and by we're go - ing home.
O sin - ner, to the Saviour come, And join the band that's go - ing home.

CHORUS.

Go -ing home, go-ing home, How sweet the thought we're go - ing home.

OLD HUNDRED. Doxology.

Praise God, from whom all blessings flow ; Praise Him, all creatures here be - low ;

Praise Him a - bove, ye heavenly host ; Praise Fa-ther, Son, and Ho-ly Ghost.

100

ONE BY ONE.

Words by E. Rinehart.   Music by Asa Hull.

Andante, espressivo.

1. One by one are au - tumn leaves Borne a - way on win-try breeze;
2. One by one the stars of night Dis - ap - pear with morning light;

Thus we pass from earth a - way, This life is fleet - ing as a day.
Thus the fee - ble, earth - ly ray Is lost in blaze of end - less day.

CHORUS.

One by one,........ one by one,............ One by one we pass a - way,

One by one,   one by one,

This life is fleet-ing as a day, This life is fleet-ing as a day.

3 One by one are voices hushed,
  Earthly joys and hopes are crushed ;
  Both the timid and the brave
  Are laid within the silent grave.
  One by one they pass away, etc.

4 One by one our friends pass o'er
  To the bright and peaceful shore ;
  And they join in glad surprise
  The glorious anthem of the skies.
  One by one they pass away, etc.

Copyright, 1879, *by* Asa Hull.

Moderato.   Words and Music by H. S. BLUNT.

1. Bro-ther, is thy path-way clouded? Does thy sun re-fuse to shine?
2. Hast thou failed to do thy du-ty? Didst thou in-to er-ror stray?

Is thy sky in darkness shrouded? Dost thou in thy sor-row pine?
There are bles-sings with-out num-ber, Christ is off-'ring thee to-day.

CHORUS.

Look up, wea-ry, faint-ing brother, See! the dawn-ing doth ap-pear;

From the east the light is breaking, Night recedes, the day is near.

3 Look, my brother, Christ is ready,
Cast on Him your every care;
Now He waits to bear your burdens,
And will all your sorrows share.
Cho.—Look up, etc.

4 See! a golden crown is waiting—
Waiting for thee over there,
Studded with the gems of heaven,
If for Christ the cross you bear.
Cho.—Look up, etc.

DUET OR QUARTETTE.   From "Praise Songs."   Music by ASA HULL.

1. What tho' the fig-tree blossoms not, Nor fruits a-dorn the ol-ive grove?
2. 'Tis sure-ly in His love a-lone The Lord our God His judgment sends;

What tho' it be my fear-ful lot, 'Midst bar-ren vines and fields to rove?
In all His ways is mer-cy shown, Throughout the earth's remotest ends.

SEMI-CHORUS.

Tho' bleat-ing flocks no more I see, Nor herds with-in the stall ap-pear;
So let us then our banners raise, To all the world His love proclaim;

Yet, still in God my trust shall be, I'll serve Him more from love than fear.
The God of our sal-va-tion praise, With triumph in His ho-ly name.

CHORUS.

Oh, praise His name! His glories sing! Ce-les-tial joy shall tune your voice;

ff

Be-hold He reigns your God and King, In Him rejoice! in Him re-joice!

3.

What though thro' death's dominion lies
  The path that leads to yonder rest,
Yet, still my song of praise shall rise
  To Him whose hand my soul hath blest.
Yea, though I pass the shade of death,
  With clouds and darkness overcast,
I'll praise Him with my latest breath,
  For O, He loves us to the last.

4.

I know that my Redeemer lives ;
  I know that He ascends on high ;
In love His children He forgives,
  And wipes the tears from ev'ry eye.
Hosanna to His name I'll sing,
  In whom such goodness I have found ;
My light, my joy, my everything ;
  Let saints and men His praise resound.

TRUSTING.

Words by Rev. WM. McDONALD.

Music by WM. G. FISCHER.

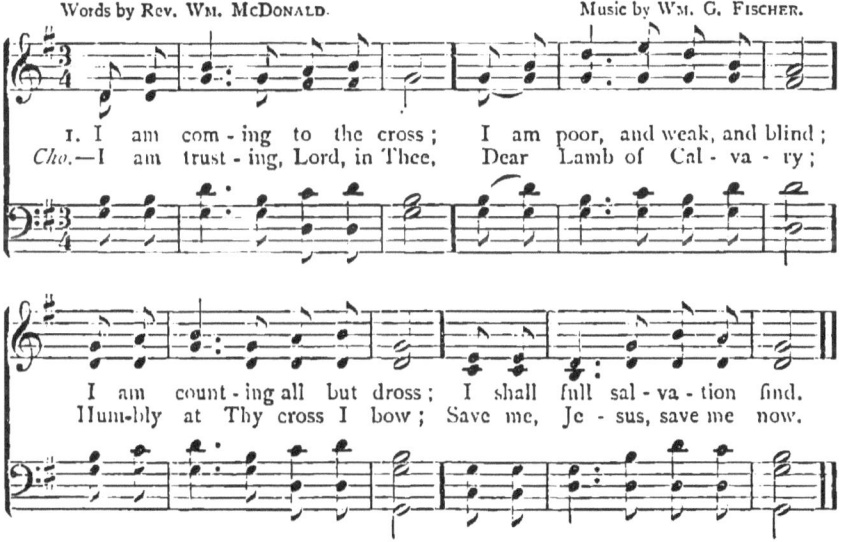

1. I am com-ing to the cross ; I am poor, and weak, and blind ;
Cho.—I am trust-ing, Lord, in Thee, Dear Lamb of Cal-va-ry ;

I am count-ing all but dross ; I shall full sal-va-tion find.
Hum-bly at Thy cross I bow ; Save me, Je-sus, save me now.

2 Long my heart has sighed for Thee ;
  Long has evil reigned within ;
Jesus sweetly speaks to me,
  I will cleanse you from all sin.—Cho.

3 Here I give my all to Thee,—
  Friends, and time, and earthly store ;
Soul and body Thine to be—
  Wholly Thine—forever more.—Cho.

4 In the promises I trust ;
  Now I feel the blood applied ;
I am prostrate in the dust ;
  I with Christ am crucified.—Cho.

5 Jesus comes ! He fills my soul !
  Perfected in love I am ;
I am every whit made whole ;
  Glory, glory to the Lamb.—Cho.

THE NEW SONG.

Words by FLORA L. BEST.

Music by JNO. R. SWENEY.

1. There are songs of joy that I loved to sing, When my heart was as blithe as a
2. There are strains of home that are dear as life, And I list to them oft 'mid the

bird... in spring ; But the song I have learn'd is so full of cheer, That the
din.... of strife ; But I know of a home that is won-drous fair, And I

CHORUS. *A little faster.*

dawn shines out in the dark-ness drear, O, the new, new song, O, the
sing the psalm they are sing-ing there. O, the new, new song,

new, new song, I can sing it now With the
O, the new, new song, I can sing just now With the

ran - - - som'd throng: Pow-er and do - min-ion to Him that shall
ransom'd, the ransom'd throng:

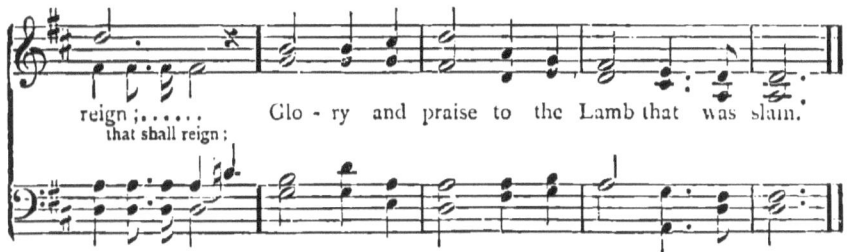

reign ;...... Glo - ry and praise to the Lamb that was slain.
that shall reign ;

3 Can my lips be mute, or my heart be sad,
  When the gracious Master hath made me glad?
  When He points where the many bright mansions be,
  And sweetly says, " There is one for thee ?"—*Chorus.*

4 I shall catch the gleam of its jasper wall,
  When I come to the gloom of the even fall,
  For I know that the shadows so dreary and dim,
  Have a path of light that will lead to Him.—*Chorus.*

MARTYN. 7s.

Words by C. WESLEY.
Andante.   Music arranged from S. B. MARSH.
                                                        Fine.

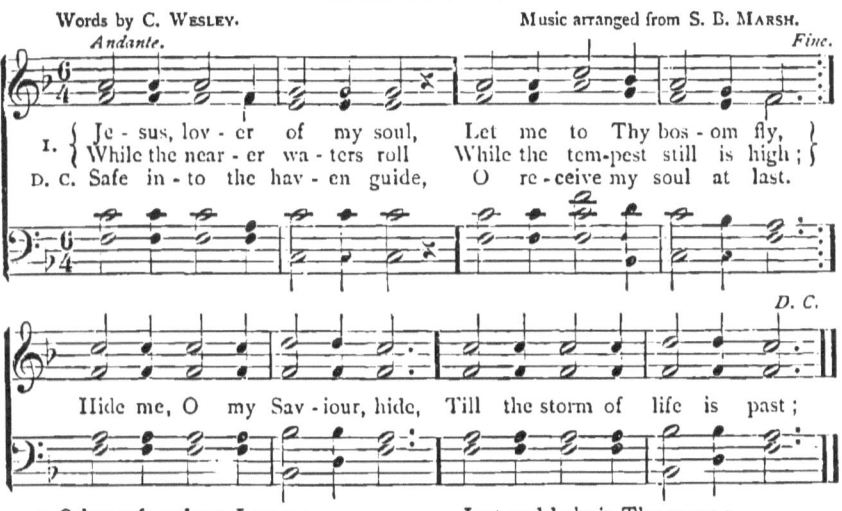

1. { Je - sus, lov - er of my soul, Let me to Thy bos - om fly, }
   { While the near - er wa - ters roll While the tem-pest still is high ; }
D. C. Safe in - to the hav - en guide, O re - ceive my soul at last.

Hide me, O my Sav - iour, hide, Till the storm of life is past ;

2 Other refuge have I none ;
  Hangs my helpless soul on Thee :
  Leave, O leave me not alone ;
  Still support and comfort me :
  All my trust on Thee is stay'd ;
  All my hope from Thee I bring ;
  Cover my defenceless head
  With the shadow of Thy wing.

3 Thou, O Christ, art all I want :
  More than all in Thee I find :
  Raise the fallen, cheer the faint,
  Heal the sick, and lead the blind.

Just and holy is Thy name ;
  I am all unrighteousness ;
  False, and full of sin I am ;
  Thou art full of truth and grace.

4 Plenteous grace with Thee is found,
  Grace to cover all my sin :
  Let the healing streams abound ;
  Make and keep me pure within.
  Thou of life the fountain art ;
  Freely let me take of Thee :
  Spring Thou up within my heart ;
  Rise to all eternity.

Legato.

Music by ASA HULL.

1. When we hear the mu - sic ring-ing In the bright ce - les - tial dome;
2. When the ho - ly an - gels meets us, As we go to join their band,

When sweet an-gel voi - ces sing-ing, Glad-ly bids us wel-come home;
Shall we know the friends that greet us In the glo-rious spir - it land?

To the land of an-cient sto - ry, Where the spir - it knows no care,
Shall we see the same eyes shin-ing On us, as in days of yore?

In that land of light and glo - ry, Shall we know each oth - er there?
Shall we feel their dear arms twin-ing Fond-ly round us, as be - fore?

CHORUS.

1st time. 2d time.

Shall we know, shall we know, shall we know each other there? there?
Shall we know each oth-er there? Shall we know each oth - er there? oth - er there?

Copyright, 1879, *by* ASA HULL.

Words by Mrs. E. W. Chapman.   Music by J. H. Tenney.

1. I think of yon bright mansion, Within the jas-per walls, And then I think of
2. I read of streets all golden, Of gates of precious stone, But nought to me so
3. I know that my dear Saviour Will ope, with golden key, The gates so bright and

CHORUS.

Je - sus, Who reign - eth o - ver all.   On Je - sus, the sure founda - tion,
pre - cious, As God's be-lov - ed Son.
pear - ly, At last for you and me.

Brok - en and cleft for me; Rest - ing in sweet-ness, And full completeness,

I wait till He calls for me.

4 One look of life from Jesus
   Will fill my raptured soul
   With joy and heav'nly sweetness,
   Beyond my heart's control.—*Cho.*

5 One smile of recognition,
   To show that I am His,
   Will be a full fruition,
   A perfect sea of bliss.—*Cho.*

Copyright, 1879, *by* Asa Hull.

CONCLUSION OF **THE SPIRIT'S WELCOME,** OPPOSITE PAGE.

3 Yes, my earth-worn soul rejoices,
   And my weary heart grows light ;
   For the thrilling angel voices,
   And the angel faces bright
   That shall welcome us in heaven
   Are the loved of long ago,
   And to them 'tis kindly given,
   Thus their mortal friends to know.
   Chorus.—We shall know, etc.

4 O, ye weary, sad, and tossed ones,
   Droop not, faint not by the way ;
   Ye shall join the loved and lost ones
   In the land of perfect day !
   Harp-strings touched by angel fingers
   Murmured in my raptured ear ;
   Evermore their sweet song lingers—
   " We shall know each other there."
   Chorus.—We shall know, etc.

RESTING AT THE CROSS.

Music by Wm. J. Kirkpatrick.

1. To the cross of Christ, my Sav-iour, I had brought my weary soul,
2. At the cross, while meekly bow-ing, Je-sus, smiling, bade me live;

Burden'd, faint, and broken-hearted, Pray-ing, "Je-sus, make me whole."
I have died for your transgressions, And I free-ly all for-give.

CHORUS.

Glo-ry, glo-ry be to Je-sus, I am counting all but dross,

I have found a full sal-va-tion, I am rest-ing at the cross;

I'm rest-ing, I'm rest-ing, I'm rest-ing at the cross.
at the cross, at the cross,

THE GREAT PHYSICIAN.  109

Arranged by Rev. J. H. Stockton.

1. The great Phy-si-cian now is near, The sym-pa-thiz-ing Je - sus;
2. Your ma - ny sins are all forgiven, Oh, hear the voice of Je - sus;
3. All glo - ry to the dy - ing Lamb ! I now be-lieve in Je - sus;

He speaks the drooping heart to cheer, Oh, hear the voice of Je - sus.
Go on your way in peace to heaven, And wear a crown with Je - sus.
I love the bless - ed Saviour's name, I love the name of Je - sus.

CHORUS.

Sweet - est note of ser - aph song, Sweet-est name on mor - tal tongue,

Sweet - est car - ol ev - er sung, Je - sus, bless - ed Je - sus.

4 His name dispels my guilt and fear,
No other name but Jesus ;
Oh, how my soul delights to hear
The precious name of Jesus.—*Cho.*

5 And when to that bright world above,
We rise to see our Jesus,
We'll sing around the throne of love
His name, the name of Jesus.—*Cho.*

CONCLUSION OF **RESTING AT THE CROSS,** OPPOSITE PAGE.

3 At the cross, while prostrate lying,
Jesus' blood flowed o'er my soul ;
All my guilt and sin were covered,
And He whispered, " Child, be whole."

4 At the cross I'm calmly trusting ;
Every moment now is sweet ;
I am tasting of His glory ;
I am resting at His feet.

Words and Melody by Rev. R. H. MCRAV.

1. We shall meet in that beautiful land, On the banks of the bright golden shore,
2. O-ver there on the bright azure plains, Where the riv-er of life sweetly flows;

And with all the redeemed spirit-band, There with Je-sus to reign ev-er more.
For the Sav-iour e-ter-nal-ly reigns, And the beau-ti-ful gates never close.

CHORUS.

In a bright, happy home, we shall meet, In that beau-ti-ful, beau-ti-ful
we shall meet,

land,......... In a bright, hap-py home we shall meet,...... In that
beau-ti-ful land,   we shall meet,

beau-ti-ful, beau-ti-ful land.
beautiful land.

3 Blessed Jesus has gone to prepare
  Us a crown that is brighter than day;
  Then forever we'll dwell with Him there,
  And His hand shall wipe all tears away.

4 There no sorrow shall e'er taint the air,
  Where God dwells evil never can come;
  And no weeping will break on the ear,
  When the day of life's turmoil is done.

Words by Edgar Page.　　　From "Goodly Pearls."　Music by Jno. R. Sweney.

1. I've reached the land of corn and wine, And all its rich - es free - ly mine;
2. My Sav - iour comes and walks with me, And sweet communion here have we,
3. A sweet per-fume up - on the breeze Is borne from ev - er - ver - nal trees,
4. The zep-hyrs seem to float to me Sweet sounds of heaven's mel - o - dy,

Here shines undimm'd one blissful day, For all my night has pass'd a - way.
He gen - tly leads me by His hand, For this is heav - en's bor - der - land.
And flow'rs that nev - er - fad - ing grow Where streams of life for - ev - er flow.
As an - gels with the white-robed throng Join in the sweet re - demption song.

CHORUS.

O Beu - lah Land, sweet Beulah Land, As on thy high - est mount I stand,

I look a - way a - cross the sea, Where mansions are pre-pared for me,

And view the shin - ing glo - ry shore, My heav'n, my home, for ev - er-more!

LIVE NEARER TO JESUS.

Words and Music by Alex. S. Arnold.

1. Live nearer to Je - sus, Trusting ev-er in Him ; He waiteth to free us
2. Live nearer to Je - sus, Ev-er trust in His pow'r ; Thro' life He will lead us,
3. Live nearer to Je - sus, And His Spirit re - ceive ; He'll never deceive us—

From the bondage of sin. Stand up for the Saviour, Stand up ever for Him ;
Cheering ev'ry dark hour. Stray not from His keeping, In Him always abide ;
O, His promise be-lieve. Sweet is the communion, Yes, more precious than gold ;

Rit. ad lib.   CHORUS. *A tempo.*

In du-ty ne'er waver, He is Saviour and King. In His love we're stronger,
Joys constant-ly reaping, Clinging close to His side.
In heaven-ly u - nion We His beauty behold.

In His strength we conquer ; Trust in self no longer, Trust Thy Saviour and King.

Music by Asa Hull.

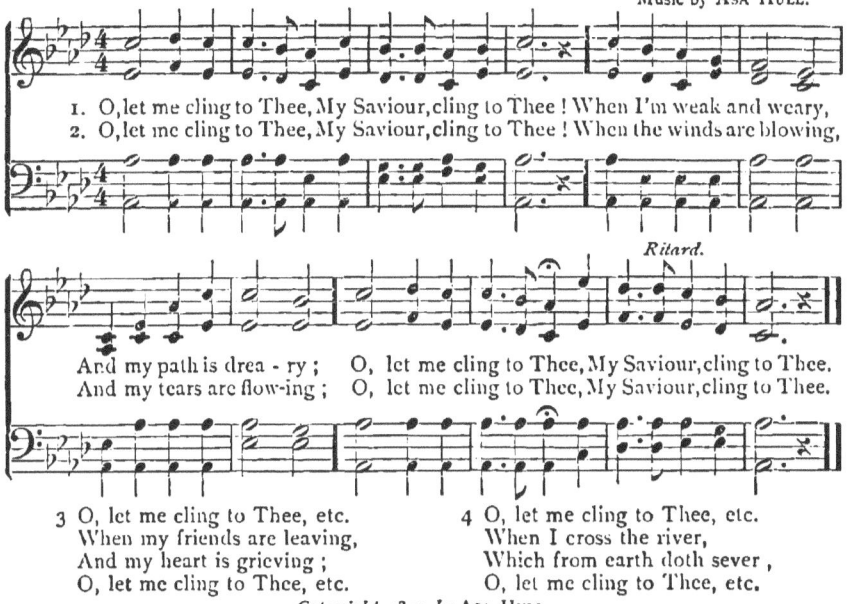

1. O, let me cling to Thee, My Saviour, cling to Thee ! When I'm weak and weary,
2. O, let me cling to Thee, My Saviour, cling to Thee ! When the winds are blowing,

And my path is drea - ry ; O, let me cling to Thee, My Saviour, cling to Thee.
And my tears are flow-ing ; O, let me cling to Thee, My Saviour, cling to Thee.

3 O, let me cling to Thee, etc.
When my friends are leaving,
And my heart is grieving ;
O, let me cling to Thee, etc.

4 O, let me cling to Thee, etc.
When I cross the river,
Which from earth doth sever ,
O, let me cling to Thee, etc.

BOYLSTON. S. M.

Words by C. Wesley.   Music by L. Mason.

1. A charge to keep I have, A God to glo - ri - fy,
2. To serve the pres - ent age, My call - ing to ful - fill ;

A nev - er - dy - ing soul to save, And fit it for the sky.
O, may it all my powers en - gage To do my Mas - ter's will.

3 Arm me with jealous care,
As in Thy sight to live ;
And O, Thy servant, Lord, prepare
A strict account to give.

4 Help me to watch and pray,
And on Thyself rely,
Assured, if I my trust betray,
I shall forever die.

THE BEAUTIFUL VALE.

Words arr. by Asa Hull.

Music by Asa Hull.

Soli. *mp* Tutti. *f*

1. My soul with rap - ture waits for thee, Beau-ti - ful vale of rest;
2. Thy ra - diant fields and glow-ing skies, Beau-ti - ful vale of rest;

Soli. *mp* Tutti. *f*

My home be - yond the roll - ing sea, Beau - ti - ful vale of rest;
Too pure and bright for mor - tal eyes, Beau - ti - ful vale of rest;

Soli. *A little slower.*

I long to sing thy pleas - ures o'er, The beau - ties of thy tranquil shore,
Be - side the liv - ing stream that flows, The wea - ry heart that finds re - pose;

Tutti. *A tempo.*

Where pain and sor - row comes no more, Beau - ti - ful vale of rest.
Thy pearl - y gates shall nev - er close, Beau - ti - ful vale of rest.

CHORUS.

Beau-ti-ful vale...... of rest, Beau-ti-ful vale...... of rest,
Beau-ti-ful vale of rest, Beau-ti-ful vale of rest.

My soul with rapture waits for thee, O beau-ti-ful vale of rest!

3.
The joys of earth, how soon they fade!
  Beautiful vale of rest ;
Like morning dew or evening shade,
  Beautiful vale of rest ;
Yet when we reach thy golden strand,
Our gentle Saviour's promised land,
We'll sing with all the ransomed band,—
  Beautiful vale of rest.

4.
O, who would dwell for ever here,
  Beautiful vale of rest ;
With joy, unfading joy, so near?
  Beautiful vale of rest ;
O, may I live, that I may wear
A starry crown for ever there,
And breathe thy sweet and balmy air,
  Beautiful vale of rest.

THE CLEANSING FOUNTAIN.

Words by WILLIAM COWPER.   Western Melody.

1. { There is a foun-tain filled with blood Drawn from Im-man-uel's veins ;
{ And sin-ners plunged beneath that flood, [OMIT....................]

D. C. And sin-ners plunged beneath that flood, [OMIT....................]

Lose all their guilty stains. Lose all their guilty stains, Lose all their guilty stains.

Lose all their guilty stains.

2 The dying thief rejoiced to see
  That fountain in his day ;
And there may I, though vile as he,
  Wash all my sins away.

3 Thou dying Lamb ! Thy precious blood
  Shall never lose its power,
Till all the ransomed Church of God,
  Are saved, to sin no more.

4 E'er since, by faith, I saw the stream,
  The flowing wounds supply,
Redeeming love has been my theme,
  And shall be, till I die.

5 Then in a nobler, sweeter song,
  I'll sing Thy power to save,
When this poor, lisping, stamm'ring
  Lies silent in the grave.   [tongue,

116   **COMPANIONSHIP WITH JESUS.**

Words by Mary D. James.   Music by Wm. J. Kirkpatrick.

Words by Rev. Jos. H. GILMORE.

Music by Wm. B. BRADBURY.

1. He lead - eth me! O bless-ed thought, O, words of heav'nly comfort fraught;
2. Sometimes 'mid scenes of deepest gloom, Sometimes when Eden's bowers bloom,

What - e'er I do, wher-e'er I be, Still 'tis God's hand that lead-eth me.
By wa - ters still, o'er troubled sea,—Still 'tis His hand that lead-eth me.

CHORUS.

He lead-eth me! He lead-eth me! By His own hand He lead-eth me;

His faith-ful follower I would be, For by His hand He lead-eth me.

3 Lord, I would clasp Thy hand in mine,
Nor ever murmur nor repine—
Content, whatever lot I see,
Since 'tis my God that leadeth me.
Chorus.—He leadeth me, etc.

4 And when my task on earth is done,
When, by Thy grace, the victory's won,
E'en death's cold wave I will not flee,
Since God through Jordan leadeth me.
Chorus.—He leadeth me, etc.

By permission of BIGLOW & MAIN.

Words by Dr. H. Bonar.

Music by C. C. Converse.

1. What a friend we have in Je - sus,   All our sins and griefs to bear ;

What a priv - i - lege to car - ry   Ev - 'ry - thing to Him in prayer.

O, what peace we oft - en for - feit,   O, what need-less pain we bear ;

All be-cause we do not car - ry   Ev - 'ry - thing to Him in prayer.

2 Have we trials and temptations ?
   Is there trouble anywhere ?
We should never be discouraged,
   Take it to the Lord in prayer.
Can we find a friend so faithful,
   Who will all our sorrows share ?
Jesus knows our ev'ry weakness,
   Take it to the Lord in prayer.

3 Are we weak and heavy-laden,
   Cumbered with a load of care,
Precious Saviour, still our refuge,
   Take it to the Lord in prayer.
Do thy friends despise, forsake thee,
   Take it to the Lord in prayer ;
In His arms He'll take and shield thee,
   Thou wilt find a solace there.

Words by C. Wesley.

Music by Jos. P. Holbrook. By per.

1. Je-sus, lov-er of my soul, Let me to Thy bo-som fly,
2. Oth-er ref-uge have I none, Hangs my help-less soul on Thee;

While the near-er wa-ters roll, While the tem-pest still is high;
Leave, O, leave me not a-lone, Still sup-port and com-fort me:

FULL CHORUS.

Hide me, O my Sav-iour, hide, Till the storm of life is past;
All my trust on Thee is stayed, All my help from Thee I bring;

Safe in-to the ha-ven guide, O, re-ceive my soul at last.
Cov-er my de-fence-less head With the shad-ow of Thy wing

3 Thou, O Christ, art all I want;
More than all in Thee I find:
Raise the fallen, cheer the faint,
Heal the sick, and lead the blind:
Just and holy is Thy name,
I am all unrighteousness;
Vile, and full of sin I am,
Thou art full of truth and grace.

4 Plenteous grace with Thee is found—
Grace to cover all my sin:
Let the healing streams abound;
Make me, keep me pure within.
Thou of life the Fountain art,
Freely let me take of Thee;
Spring Thou up within my heart,
Rise to all eternity.

GIVE THANKS, ALL YE PEOPLE.

Words by Dr. MUHLENBURG.

Music by ASA HULL.

With Energy.

1. Give thanks, all ye people, give thanks to the Lord, Al - le - 'lu - ias of
2. For the sunshine and rainfall, en - rich - ing a - gain   Our   a - cres in

freedom with joyful accord : Let the East and the West, North and South roll along,
myriads with treasures of grain ; For the Earth still unloading her manifold wealth,

CHORUS.

Sea, mountain, and prairie, one thanksgiving song. Give thanks, all ye people, give
For the Skies beaming vigor, the Winds breathing health.

thanks to the Lord,   Al - le - lu - ias of free-dom with joy - ful ac - cord.

3 In the Domes of Messiah, ye worshiping throngs,
   Solemn litanies mingle with jubilant songs ;
   The Ruler of Nations beseeching to spare,
   And our Union to keep the Elect of His care.—*Chorus.*

4 Our guilt and transgressions remember no more ;
   Peace, Lord ! righteous Peace, as Thy gift we adore,
   And the Banner of Union, restored by Thy Hand,
   Be the Banner of Freedom o'er all in the Land.—*Chosus.*

Music by Rev. R. LOWRY.

1. Shall we gath-er at the riv - er, Where bright angel feet have trod,
2. On the mar-gin of the riv - er, Wash-ing up its sil - ver spray,
3. Ere we reach the shining riv - er, Lay we ev - 'ry bur-den down ;

With its crys-tal tide for - ev - er Flow-ing by the throne of God.
We will walk and wor-ship ev - er, All the hap-py gold-en day.
Grace our spir - its will de - liv - er, And pro-vide a robe and crown,

CHORUS.

Yes, we'll gath-er at the riv - er, The beautiful, the beau-ti-ful riv - er ;

Gath - er with the saints at the riv - er, That flows by the throne of God.

4 At the smiling of the river,
    Mirror of the Saviour's face,
Saints whom death will never sever,
    Lift their songs of saving grace.
    Cho.—Yes, we'll gather, etc.

5 Soon we'll reach the silver river ;
    Soon our pilgrimage will cease ;
Soon our happy hearts will quiver
    With the melody of peace.
    Cho.—Yes, we'll gather, etc.

JUST AS I AM.

Words by CHARLOTTE ELLIOTT.　　　　　Music by WM. B. BRADBURY.

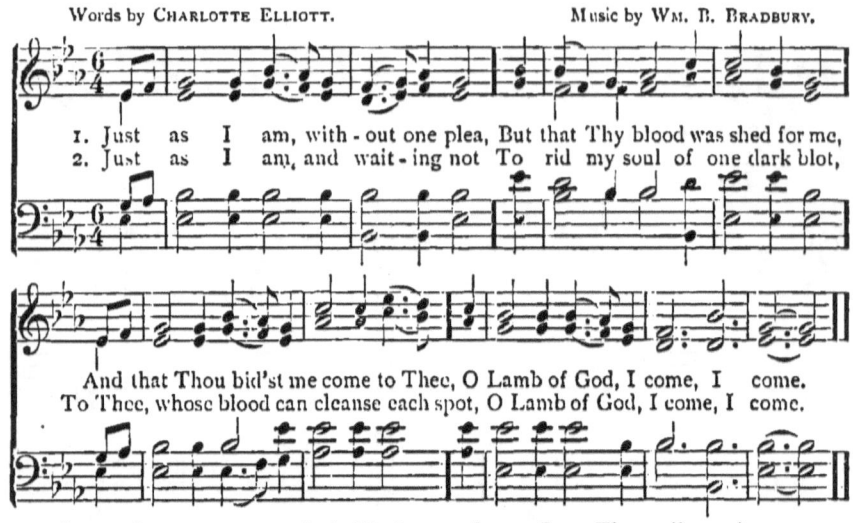

1. Just as I am, with-out one plea, But that Thy blood was shed for me,
2. Just as I am, and wait-ing not To rid my soul of one dark blot,

And that Thou bid'st me come to Thee, O Lamb of God, I come, I come.
To Thee, whose blood can cleanse each spot, O Lamb of God, I come, I come.

3 Just as I am, poor, wretched, blind,
　Sight, riches, healing of the mind,
　Yea, all I need in Thee I find ;
　　O Lamb of God, I come, I come.

4 Just as I am, though toss'd about,
　With many a conflict, many a doubt,
　Fightings within, and fears without,—
　　O Lamb of God, I come, I come.

5 Just as I am Thou wilt receive,
　Wilt welcome, pardon, cleanse, relieve ;
　Because Thy promise I believe,
　　O Lamb of God, I come, I come.

6 Just as I am, Thy love unknown
　Has broken every barrier down ;
　Now to be Thine, yea, Thine alone,
　　O Lamb of God, I come, I come.

DENNIS. S. M.

Words by JOHN FAWCETT.　　　　　Arranged from NAGELI.

1. Blest be the tie that binds Our hearts in Chris-tian love ;
2. Be - fore our Fa - ther's throne We pour our ar - dent prayers ;

The fel - low - ship of kin -dred minds Is like to that a - bove.
Our fears, our hopes, our aims are one, Our com - forts and our cares.

Words by H. Bonar. Music by Asa Hull.

1. I heard the voice of Je-sus say, "Come un-to me and rest:
Lay down, thou wea-ry one, lay down Thy head up-on my breast."

I came to Je-sus as I was, Wea-ry, and worn, and sad;

I found in Him a rest-ing place, And He has made me glad.

2 I heard the voice of Jesus say,
   " Behold, I freely give
The living water : thirsty one,
   Stoop down and drink, and live."
I came to Jesus, and I drank
   Of that life-giving stream ;
My thirst was quench'd, my soul revived,
   And now I live in Him.

3 I heard the voice of Jesus say,
   " I am this dark world's light ;
Look unto Me, thy morn shall rise,
   And all thy day be bright."
I looked to Jesus, and I found
   In Him my Star, my Sun ;
And in that light of life I'll walk,
   Till trav'ling days are done.

Copyright, 1871, by Asa Hull.

CONCLUSION OF **DENNIS,** OPPOSITE PAGE.

3 We share our mutual woes ;
   Our mutual burdens bear ;
And often for each other flows
   The symphathizing tear.

4 When we asunder part,
   It gives us inward pain ;
But we shall still be join'd in heart,
   And hope to meet again.

5 This glorious hope revives
   Our courage by the way ;
While each in expectation lives,
   And longs to see the day.

6 From sorrow, toil, and pain,
   And sin we shall be free ;
And perfect love and friendship reign
   Through all eternity.

SICILIAN HYMN.

Words by WALTER SHIRLEY.

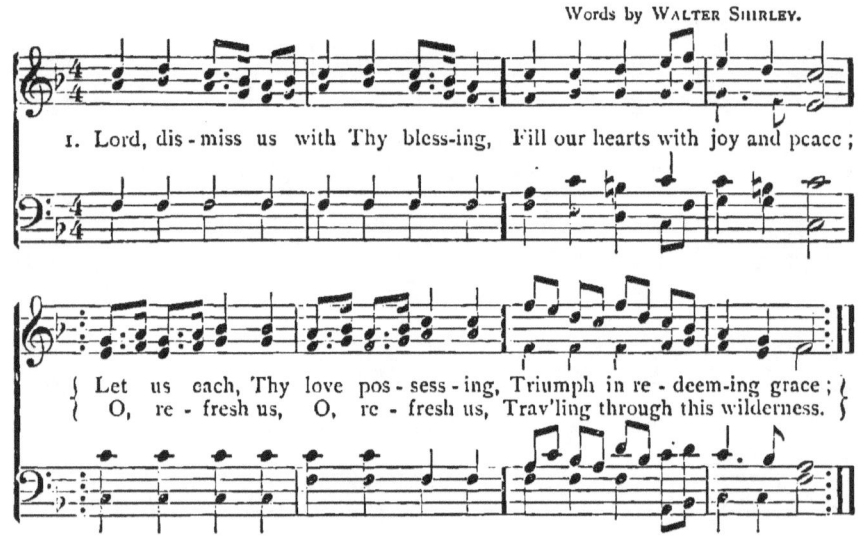

1. Lord, dis-miss us with Thy bless-ing, Fill our hearts with joy and peace;

Let us each, Thy love pos-sess-ing, Triumph in re-deem-ing grace;
O, re-fresh us, O, re-fresh us, Trav'ling through this wilderness.

2 Thanks we give, and adoration,
For Thy gospel's joyful sound ;
May the fruits of Thy salvation
In our hearts and lives abound :
:‖: May Thy presence :‖:
With us evermore be found.

3 So, where'er the signal's given
Us from earth to call away,
Borne on angels' wings to heaven,
Glad the summons to obey,
:‖: May we ever :‖:
Reign with Christ in endless day.

OLIVET.

Words by RAY PALMER.   Music by L. MASON.

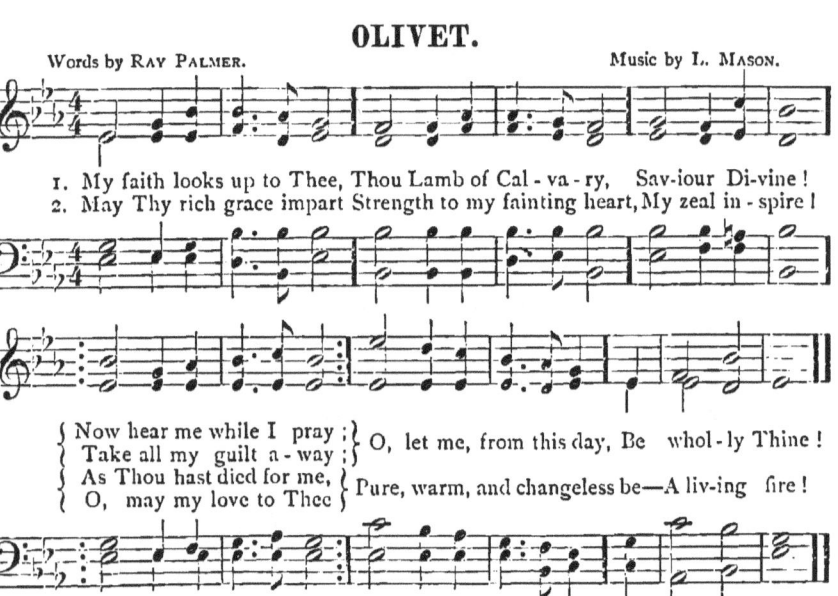

1. My faith looks up to Thee, Thou Lamb of Cal-va-ry, Sav-iour Di-vine !
2. May Thy rich grace impart Strength to my fainting heart, My zeal in-spire !

Now hear me while I pray ;
Take all my guilt a-way ;
As Thou hast died for me,
O, may my love to Thee

O, let me, from this day, Be whol-ly Thine !
Pure, warm, and changeless be—A liv-ing fire !

Words by JAMES ALLEN.   Music by ASA HULL.

1. Sweet the mo-ments, rich in bless-ing, Which be-fore the cross I spend;

Life and health and peace pos-sess-ing From the sin-ner's dy-ing Friend;
D. S. Still in faith and hope a-bid-ing, Life de-riv-ing from His death.

Love and grief my heart di-vid-ing, With my tears His feet I'll bathe;

2 O, how blessed is the station,
  Low before the cross to lie,
While I see divine compassion
Beaming from His gracious eye;
Here I'll sit forever, viewing
Mercy streaming in His blood:
Precious drops my soul bedewing,
Plead and claim my peace with God.

3 Here it is I find my heaven,
  While upon the Lamb I gaze;
Here I see my sins forgiven,
Lost in wonder, love and praise:
May I still enjoy this feeling,
In all need to Jesus go,
Prove each day His blood more healing,
And Himself more deeply know.

CONCLUSION OF **OLIVET**, OPPOSITE PAGE.

3 While life's dark maze I tread,
  And griefs around me spread,
    Be Thou my guide;
  Bid darkness turn to day,
  Wipe sorrow's tears away,
  Nor let me ever stray
    From Thee aside.

4 When ends life's transient dream,
  When death's cold, sullen stream
    Shall o'er me roll,
  Blest Saviour! then, in love,
  Fear and distrust remove;
  O, bear me safe above—
    A ransomed soul!

INDEX OF TUNES.

INDEX OF HYMNS.